The Road to a Hunger-Free America

The Road to a Hunger-Free America

Selected Writings of Mark Winne

MARK WINNE

BLOOMSBURY ACADEMIC
NEW YORK • LONDON • OXFORD • NEW DELHI • SYDNEY

BLOOMSBURY ACADEMIC

Bloomsbury Publishing Inc, 1359 Broadway, New York, NY 10018, USA
Bloomsbury Publishing Plc, 50 Bedford Square, London, WC1B 3DP, UK
Bloomsbury Publishing Ireland, 29 Earlsfort Terrace, Dublin 2, D02 AY28, Ireland

BLOOMSBURY, BLOOMSBURY ACADEMIC and the Diana logo
are trademarks of Bloomsbury Publishing Plc

First published in the United States of America 2025

Copyright © Mark Winne, 2025

Cover image: Trees on field © Devin Johnson/Getty

All rights reserved. No part of this publication may be: i) reproduced or transmitted in any form, electronic or mechanical, including photocopying, recording or by means of any information storage or retrieval system without prior permission in writing from the publishers; or ii) used or reproduced in any way for the training, development or operation of artificial intelligence (AI) technologies, including generative AI technologies. The rights holders expressly reserve this publication from the text and data mining exception as per Article 4(3) of the Digital Single Market Directive (EU) 2019/790.

Bloomsbury Publishing Inc does not have any control over, or responsibility for, any third-party websites referred to or in this book. All internet addresses given in this book were correct at the time of going to press. The author and publisher regret any inconvenience caused if addresses have changed or sites have ceased to exist, but can accept no responsibility for any such changes.

A catalog record for this book is available from the Library of Congress.

ISBN: HB: 979-8-7651-3235-7
PB: 979-8-7651-3234-0
ePDF: 979-8-7651-3236-4
eBook: 979-8-7651-3237-1

Typeset by Integra Software Services Pvt. Ltd.
Printed and bound in the United States of America

For product safety related questions contact productsafety@bloomsbury.com.

To find out more about our authors and books visit www.bloomsbury.com and sign up for our newsletters.

This book is dedicated to the 1001 people I have met along the road to a hunger-free America whose faith in justice, dedication to the task, and shimmering imaginations have inspired me every step of the way. You are the warriors, workers, and weavers who will make the dream come true.

Old men delight in giving good advice as a consolation for the fact that they can no longer set bad examples.
FRANÇOIS DE LA ROCHEFOUCAULD

CONTENTS

List of Contributors xi
Foreword by Sara Elnakib xii

Introduction: Mapping the Journey; Building the Foundation 1

PART ONE Places 25
1 Great Falls, Great Food, Great Gaps: The Tale of Paterson and Ridgewood 27
2 New Roots Community Farm: "This is the coolest place I've ever been!" 39
3 Laredo Shows the Way to a Mending Wall 47
4 Roadkill Stew, Bad-ass Cabbage, and the Midnight Sun—Lessons from Alaska 57
5 Huerta del Valle—An Ontario Oasis 63
6 Where's the Rage? 69
7 Troubled by Paradise 75
8 Israel's War on Palestinian Olive Farmers 81

PART TWO People 87
9 A Rainbow of Farmers 89

10 I Have Seen the Future of Medicine: It Is Dr. Yum 97
11 It's Not Easy Being a Commercial Egg Farmer 103
12 My Dinner with Embry 109
13 New Jersey = Tomato 117
14 "I'm Tired of Watching Our Town Die" 127
15 Two Million Angry Moms and One Sociologist: *Free For All: Fixing School Food in America* 137
16 George McGovern: A Man Ahead of His Time 143

PART THREE Actions 147

17 When Handouts Keep Coming, the Food Line Never Ends 149
18 Welcome to the Weight Wars 155
19 Love in the Time of Corona 165
20 The Poetry of Community Food Assessments 171
21 Food Co-ops: A Faith Renewed 177
22 Twenty-Five Years of Food Security, Good Food, and Empowerment 183
23 The Most Important Word in "Community Gardening" is not "Gardening"! 189

Conclusion: The Journey Continues; The Tasks Are Clear 197

References 202
Index 206

CONTRIBUTORS

Mark Winne has been active in the US food movement for fifty-five years as a non-profit food organization director, organizer, policy advocate, and writer. For twenty-five years he ran the Hartford Food System in Connecticut and, more recently, served as a senior advisor to the Center for a Livable Future at Johns Hopkins University. He is the author of five books and blogs regularly at markwinne.com. Mark lives and writes in Santa Fe, New Mexico.

Sara Elnakib is an educator, associate professor, and chair of the Department of Family and Community Health Sciences at Rutgers Cooperative Extension. Her research and community work centers on advancing child health equity and environmental stewardship through policy, systems, and environmental change strategies, with a focus on schools and community-based settings.

Sara's work has been supported by the USDA, EPA, NJDEP, and the Horizon Foundation, exploring the intersection of nutrition literacy, environmental education, and healthy eating. Her doctoral research examined strategies to reduce food waste in schools by applying behavioral economics principles.

Sara earned her doctorate in Social and Behavioral Health Sciences from the Rutgers School of Public Health. She is a Registered Dietitian Nutritionist and holds a Master of Public Health degree in Health Education and Behavioral Sciences from the University of Medicine and Dentistry of New Jersey, as well as a bachelor's degree in Nutritional Sciences from Rutgers University.

Sara is passionate about creating healthier, more sustainable communities through research, education, and collaborative action.

FOREWORD

By Sara Elnakib, PhD, MPH, RDN

Mark Winne's writings have been a source of inspiration and guidance to me for many years. His essays and books opened my eyes to the complex web of food justice and the potential of collaborative solutions like food policy councils to transform systems. Mark has a rare ability to highlight both the challenges and the hope within our food systems. His work serves as a beacon, especially for those engaged in food justice, where the road often feels steep and lonely. His essays remind us that change is possible when motivated people unite with a shared purpose.

In *The Road to a Hunger-Free America*, Mark brings to life the extraordinary power of people, places, and actions to create meaningful transformation. He masterfully intertwines stories of grassroots efforts, systemic barriers, and the pursuit of equity, demonstrating that food is far more than sustenance—a connector, a divider, and a potential equalizer.

What sets this collection apart is its emphasis on the human dimension of food justice. In academia, we often get caught up in theories of change, frameworks, and constructs. While those have their place, Mark's essays pull us into the lived experiences of those driving local, national, and global change. He doesn't just analyze systems; he humanizes them, showcasing the individuals and communities who work tirelessly to challenge inequities and advocate for justice.

From the streets of Paterson, New Jersey, where I grew up, to the olive groves of the West Bank, Mark weaves together local and global narratives that expose the persistent need for justice and equity in our systems.

Take, for example, his story of Palestinian olive oil farmers in the West Bank, whose daily struggles under occupation highlight both the fragility and resilience of their livelihoods. Or his portrayal of community advocates in American cities, where residents of all backgrounds come together to reimagine food systems that prioritize sovereignty and sustainability. These essays are not just accounts of challenges; they are celebrations of courage, creativity, and the unyielding pursuit of justice.

As I revisited some of these essays, I was struck again by the power of collective action. Time and again, Mark shows how diverse groups of community advocates, residents, and organizations come together with an unwavering commitment to justice and equity. His work reminds me of a phrase by artist and advocate Danielle Coke that hangs in my office: "*Diversity is the fruit, and equity is the root.*" This sentiment is woven throughout Mark's essays, as he celebrates the small yet significant victories of communities fighting for food sovereignty.

This book is more than a collection of essays—it's a call to action. It challenges us to engage deeply with the systems around us and the people within them. I hope it inspires you as much as it has inspired me. Let it spark conversations, strengthen movements, and fuel your commitment to a more just and equitable food system.

Enjoy this journey through Mark's writings, and let's keep building the future he envisions—together.

Introduction: Mapping the Journey; Building the Foundation

So much of how I and others found our way into food, farm, and hunger work has been through our early encounters with injustice. There's nothing so potentially volatile, so ready to ignite a young adult's ardor than a confrontation with something that affronts their moral sensibility. They, we, and I are so emotionally charged that whatever tinder might present itself kindles passions so irrepressible that more rational or deliberate approaches fall by the wayside. Light the fuse, cover your ears against the roar, and watch the cannonballs soar!

My own cauldron started bubbling when, as an embittered eighteen-year-old, I turned in two hunting firearms to my local police station as an act of protest following the assassinations of Reverend Martin Luther King, Jr. and Robert F. Kennedy, both in the spring of 1968. A year later in college, I would organize a campus fundraiser for hunger relief in Nigeria after photographs of starving children brought me to tears. With nearly daily reports of the futility and destruction of the Vietnam War, I later turned in my Selective Service (i.e., draft) card, rejected my college student deferment, and refused to cooperate with the military induction process that followed. I would later be found guilty in a federal court of refusal to submit to induction in the armed forces and was sentenced to two years of federal probation.

My peers then—as would young people over decades to come—found multiple ways to express their frustrations with the world as they found it. College classmates would seek shelter from or oppose the Vietnam War. They would march on Washington, pray on their knees for a high draft lottery number, and occasionally take refuge in Canada. Pursuing an opposite tack, a later generation would crowd military recruitment centers to enlist as a way of opposing the injustice of the innocents who died from the September 11, 2001 terrorist attacks. Others would "occupy" Wall Street to highlight the injustice of America's atrocious income and wealth gaps. And thousands would erect tents on American campuses to demand an end to the slaughter of West Bank and Gaza Palestinians by Israeli military forces and settlers following the atrocities committed by Hamas against Israeli communities on October 7, 2023.

But to understand injustice and respond to it effectively, whether in the grand context of the human experience or in its more granular manifestations that we'll see in the essays that follow, we need more than youthful fire in the belly. Truly, no one would sing louder than me when these lines from The Clash came around, "Let fury have the hour/Anger can be power/You know that you can use it." Call it the heavy chains of aging, but I now want to know that my fury is well-grounded in fact, and that my anger is focused on the right cause and solution. And if I want to have more power, I will also want more allies whose voices are saying the same thing at more or less the same time. To those ends, commonly agreed upon definitions of injustice, justice, and their respective resolutions and applications are required. For those reasons, the aim of this book is to see how the places, people, and actions of activists and projects from across the US address the challenges and opportunities presented by food system failures, especially within the context of food security, sustainability, and democracy.

What is Justice?

With an eye to providing a justice framework for our consideration of the upcoming essays—building a foundation that we can stand on—I turn to John Rawls who wrote *A Theory of Justice* in 1971. Though a vast literature on the topic of social, racial, environmental, and economic justice exists, Rawls's densely written work of over 500 pages created foundational principles of justice that enable us to understand the concept in its most basic form. It also allows us to build on those principles as well as extend them to virtually any form of injustice commonly recognized today, including those associated with our food system. I will not argue that Rawls's work necessarily offers the best discussion of the topic, but the words "justice" and "injustice" have, unfortunately, succumbed to so much overuse and dilution that they are perilously close to losing any commonly accepted meaning. For that reason, I will settle on Rawls's framework, partly because we are in need of some guardrails, and because Rawls offers the most logical process and solid arguments for understanding and applying the meaning of justice that I have encountered.

The evolution of Rawls's theory begins with a beguiling and relatively well-known scenario of a randomly selected group of people whose task it is to develop the "original principles" of justice from nothing more than the "airy nothing" of their own underlying humanity. These chosen few come from an imaginary society and are shrouded in what Rawls calls "the veil of ignorance." As such, they have no knowledge or consciousness of their own identity such as race, gender, political party, wealth, religion, or country of origin, which means that they do not bring any pre-existing self-interest(s) to the negotiating table. Nor do they possess any historical context such as awarenesses of past abuses, slights, vendettas, or the most extreme and atrocious events of centuries past that might prejudice their judgment. That same ignorance of their individual circumstances or an association with a particular community, racial, or ethnic group applies to the present as well. They do know that as human beings they will procreate, that future generations will follow them and thus be subject to the decisions they make. Hence, their implied obligation to their present society also extends well into the future.

What have these "ignorant" but wise, pre-fall-from-grace Adams and Eves decided? With more than a little help from Rawls who passes his thinking through centuries of ideas and philosophers as well as his own 1971, white, Harvard academic position, we are handed two overarching principles (I have placed verbatim quotes in italics).

First Principle: Each person is to have equal right to the most extensive total system of equal basic liberties compatible with a similar system of liberty for all. My explanation: Rich or poor, Black or white, American or Russian, every person is entitled to the same agreed upon rights. Rawls includes the possibility that such equality can be restricted, but only if it *(a) strengthens the total system of liberties shared by all; (b) a lesser liberty must be acceptable to those bound by the lesser liberty.*

Second Principle: Social and economic inequalities are to be arranged so they are both: (a) to the greatest benefit of the least advantaged, consistent with the just savings principle, and (b) attached to offices and positions open to all under conditions of fair equality of opportunity. My explanation: Those with the fewest resources and who are socially and economically disadvantaged should receive the highest priority for assistance. Though Rawls assumes that a just society exists generally within a capitalist, market-driven system, he emphasizes that the principle of justice trumps the principle of efficiency. In other words, he dismisses the economic reasoning often heard from business leaders, economists, and political conservatives who would restrict access to sufficient resources (e.g., government programs) by under-resourced groups, especially resources that significantly increase opportunities (e.g., improved education), because it would overly burden the efficient and profitable operation of institutions, businesses, and the entire economic sector. Though a tad simplistic, I might use the bumper sticker "People before Profits!" as a convenient slogan for a just society operating according to Rawls's principles.

Consistent with the just savings principle means that a determination will be made as to how much a society must set aside (save) from generation to generation—as through income and wealth taxes and transfers—to achieve justice. The US Social Security system serves as an illustration of both a partial success and a partial failure when it comes to the application of the savings principle. All those in the US work force are subject to the same payroll tax rate, 6.2 percent (self-employed persons effectively pay double), to be paid into their Social Security account. Those who earn more than $176,100 annually (the amount increases annually in accordance with the cost of living) pay only 6.2 percent on that amount and zero percent on earnings above that. In other words, someone making $15 per hour, or $31,200 annually on a 40-hour work week is paying 6.2 percent compared to 1 percent for someone making $1 million annually ($176,100 × 6.2 percent = $10,918, maximum payroll tax, which is slightly over 1 percent of $1 million). This is a highly regressive form of taxation that does not promote a just society. Albeit, a principle of savings is in force, but it is not just.

In a just system, the lower income earner might pay into Social Security, hypothetically, 1 percent, with higher-income earners paying a graduated higher rate, capped at let's say 10 percent up to $176,100, a cap itself that would be increased substantially, if not done away with entirely. At the same time, the lower income worker, upon reaching the age of eligibility, would receive annual Social Security payments much closer to those of their higher-income counterpart through a redistribution of those funds in favor of lower income beneficiaries.

An inter-generational responsibility is a thread that weaves its way through Rawls's arguments. "In following a just savings principle," Rawls posits, "each generation makes a contribution to those coming later and receives from its predecessors." While the Social Security system provides maybe the best current model of far-reaching, inter-generational public policy, a forward-looking commitment to justice shouldn't be limited to only the passing on of social and economic benefits from one generation to the next. No better contemporary example of inter-generational *in*justice exists than the looming global environmental disaster that both the current and past generations have left to their children and grandchildren. Hence, climate change and global warming, including food and agriculture's contribution to greenhouse carbon emissions, should be added to our theory of justice bucket list.

Just as we set aside a portion of our earnings in the form of payroll taxes to assure a certain quality of life and opportunities for others in the future, so must this and future generations invest current resources (a responsibility shunned by past generations) in climate change mitigating technology and other methods in hopes that humanity will survive and thrive (may we pray it's not too late). Like Ralph Waldo Emerson remarked in *The American Scholar* "we should observe some pre-established harmony ... and some preparation of stores for their [our children's] future wants, like the ... insects, who lay up food before death for the young grub they shall never see." One can only hope that today's political leaders have sympathies at least equivalent to those of such insects.

Lastly, with respect to *(b) attached to offices and positions open to all under conditions of fair equality of opportunity,* we assume that a transparent and accessible democratic process of electing representatives and political leadership who, among other duties, will work to advance these principles, is open to all and not obstructed or restricted by unjust means. Again, by way of illustration, I would submit that the *Citizens United* ruling by the US Supreme Court, that corporations are people, places those Americans without the outsized financial resources of large corporations and billionaires through their use of political action committees (PACs) at a serious disadvantage when entering the electoral process. Add in the obscenely high cost of running for public office at anything above the local level of government, and we can see an egregious violation of the principle *of fair equality of opportunity*. And, of course, we cannot take lightly the convulsive threats to justice posed by today's authoritarian political leaders who have rocked the very foundation of democracy.

Before I turn more directly to the relevance of *A Theory of Justice* to food system concerns and the essays that constitute the heart of this book, I should again remind the reader that Rawls developed his principles well over fifty years ago. While that timing might have him immersed in the debates surrounding America's civil rights movement, Rawls would only be on the cusp of both the women's and environmental movements. Even then, he does acknowledge the need to develop an application of his theory to "animals and nature," and provides ample caveats as well as invitations for others to extend, qualify, and amplify his work. In other words, Rawls's principles are not inviolable nor handed down from on high in tablet form. They are effectively a work in progress for future generations to build on. As such, we seek to apply them to food system work.

The Food System

Understanding what constitutes a *food injustice* and how best to respond to it has been a life-long pursuit of mine. A major reason, in fact, why I chose to begin writing about the food work of others was to highlight their approach to food injustices. From my own hands-on experience as well as countless observations of other people, places, and projects, I see at least four major categories worthy of the injustice label: (1) food insecurity/hunger; (2) access to healthy and affordable food (I will include diet-related health issues here); (3) the sustainability and availability of the natural resources (e.g., water, soil) that the human community relies upon for its food supply; (4) the democratic functioning of the food system, especially with respect to food production, distribution, and pricing.

Perhaps without argument, those who are food insecure are by definition disadvantaged.[1] Secondarily, they live under social and economic conditions which generally deprive them of basic liberties. The same should be said of those who do not have ready access to healthy food. Though often walking hand-in-hand with food insecurity, limited food access (e.g., living in food deserts, food swamps, or defined geographic areas where the nutritional quality of food is inadequate and/or the price of healthy food is unaffordable) are contributors to diet-related diseases such as obesity and diabetes.

People of color are disproportionately represented among those who are food insecure and diagnosed with diet-related illnesses (obesity, diabetes) at levels significantly higher than the white population. Racism must be viewed as at least a secondary, if not primary factor when considering both food insecurity and limited food access, which are also two among many causes of diet-related illnesses. Overt racist actions as well as systemic racism are traditional means that are used to deprive people of their liberties and access to normal opportunities (e.g., education, housing, public safety). The lack of equal access to those opportunities can shackle peoples' ability to feed their families, both in the short term and the long term. It should be further noted that racist policies and actions have and continue to present barriers to full participation in "offices and positions" (e.g., state legislatures,

---

[1] Food insecurity has been measured annually since the late 1990s by the US Department of Agriculture. It is a reasonably precise indicator of the number of people, broken out by various demographic categories of individuals and households, who experience varying degrees of uncertainty as to how they will secure a daily supply of food. For 2023, the most recent year of food insecurity data as of this writing, 13.5 percent, or 47.4 million people were food insecure (the rate was 12.8 percent in 2022).

the US Congress, and other institutions) that are effectively the only authorities capable of addressing and correcting those underlying disadvantages.

Continuing with the connection between injustices and the food system, we must expand Rawls's theory to the natural resources necessary to produce food. While Rawls did not specifically address what was then the newly emerging evidence that the earth's environment was at risk, he did make a tip of the hat of sorts to "animals and nature," suggesting that there were more than adequate reasons to develop a theory of justice concerning non-human creatures and inanimate forces. The present assault on the environment leading to, among other things, climate change, includes the role that food and agriculture plays (contributing about 25 percent of all greenhouse gas emissions). When coupled with the brutality inherent in factory-style livestock production and processing facilities (to say nothing of the harm those facilities do to their surrounding environments, communities, and workers), a penetrating scream for justice from both the animal kingdom and Mother Nature can be heard worldwide, as much for their own sake as for the survival of humanity. In this regard, we might best heed the words of Walt Whitman, "Whoever degrades another, degrades me; And whatever is done or said returns at last to me."

The last in our four categories of injustices from my interpretation of *A Theory of Justice* and applied to the world of food systems is democracy itself. Here, we must delve inside the very laws of economics covering our modern-day capitalist, market-driven economy to see where the injustices lie. The evolution of modern agriculture and the methods by which our food is processed and distributed over the past century or so have effectively removed them from the consumer's sight, understanding, and any form of intimate connection. Other than those moments of shallow reverence we display when checking the apples for bruises in a supermarket bin, the well-worn food movement trope, "We don't know where our food comes from" remains as true today as ever. Not only has our industrial food system left us with nothing but a plastic-wrapped, sanitized connection to our primary source of nourishment, it has left us bereft of any way to control its products, services, corporate structures, operations, or prices. It is not a stretch to compare our lack of information to the way mushrooms are cultivated: we are kept in the dark and fed manure.

In order to operate as efficiently and profitably as possible, the shrinking number of ever larger and more consolidated food corporations treat society as nothing more than a marketplace, food as only a commodity, and all of us who buy food as mere consumers. It's the pursuit of those "efficiencies" within their capitalist cocoon that leaves us starved for intimacy and hungry for democratic participation. Our individual and community-level lack of control, linked as they are to the prevalence of food insecurity, limited access to healthy and affordable food, and the mistreatment of animals and the natural world, are antithetical to the pursuit of justice. At a macro level, i.e., national and global, the only effective countervailing force to the current economic model is public policy that includes the actions (and inactions) of all levels of government, as well as large public and private institutions, that affect our food systems. Hence, the critical need for citizen/consumer participation, primarily at the policy level. At the micro level, i.e., local and state levels of government, while food policy work is also very necessary and effective (e.g., food policy councils), we see the efforts of countless hundreds of thousands of people and projects serving as a countervailing force to marketplace failures. What you will see from the stories that follow are the many ways that people attempt to regain agency and control within their respective food system.

The Larger Landscape of Injustice

Certainly, food injustice exists within a larger context of social, economic, racial, and environmental injustices as they all do within the broader principles of Rawls's original position of justice. In the US, the stark and growing social and economic divide as documented by Thomas Piketty, Robert Putnam, and others place in sharp contrast trends that over the past fifty years have marched steadily away from equality while advancing aggressively in the direction of inequality. As Rawls was publishing his tome (1971), interestingly, the US had reached its pinnacle of economic equality. Putnam convincingly demonstrates in *The Upswing* (2020) and Piketty in *Capital in the Twenty-First Century* (2014) how the gap between the rich and the poor with respect to income and wealth had steadily narrowed between 1920 and 1970. But their analysis then reveals how the decline in corporate taxes, financial regulations, and the real value of the minimum wage—all of which were imposed during that period of rising equality—declined over the next/past fifty years creating an income gap as wide as the one at the beginning of the twentieth century (Putnam, 2020). For instance, the top 1 percent of income earners in 1913 claimed 19 percent of all national income; remarkably, their share was reduced to just 8 percent by 1976; but by 2014 the one-percenters were back up to 20 percent of all pre-tax, US income (Putnam, 2020).

Putnam further spotlights a significant crossover from economic inequality to health inequality, which corresponds as well with the rise of "lifestyle," i.e., dietary health issues. He offers research from the British medical journal *The Lancet* that found over the last three or four decades, "socioeconomic gaps in survival have ... increased. Life expectancy has risen among middle-income and higher-income Americans whereas it has stagnated among poor Americans and even declined in some demographic groups" (Bor, Cohen and Galea, 2017). The important work of Anne Case and Angus Deaton, who identified a noticeable uptick in what they called "deaths of despair" among working-class whites, is also highlighted (Case and Deaton, 2020). Their work "strongly suggests that economic distress and inequality are implicated" in the rise in drug and alcohol addiction, suicide, and depression (Putnam, 2020, 43). Putnam further points out that a bipartisan US Congress Joint Economic Committee report on deaths of despair found that such deaths were at their highest (30 per 100,000 in 1910; 45 per 100,000 in 2017) during periods of greatest economic inequality. Likewise, they were at their lowest (15 per 100,000 from 1945 to 1950) during the period of rising economic equality.

Food Safety Net

Returning to the relationship between food systems and the upswings and downswings in equality, one might wonder why, during the period of such gross inequality that has taken shape since the 1970s, we didn't witness hunger running rampant across the country. The answer has two parts. The first is that severe domestic hunger *did exist* but wasn't "discovered" until the late 1960s with the aid of national media (e.g., CBS "Hunger in America" 1968) and subsequent congressional investigations. The second answer lies in the nation's emerging nutrition safety net, largely unique among developed nations as a centerpiece of a national social welfare system, that was catalyzed in part by hunger's public exposure. Federally funded and administered nutrition programs (sixteen separate ones operate today) like the Supplemental Nutrition Assistance Program (SNAP, formerly known as food stamps which began in the early 1960s), the Women, Infant, and Children Program (WIC—begun in the early 1970s), and School Meals (actually begun in 1948 but continually expanded and diversified since then) provide tens of billions of dollars of nutrition benefits annually to eligible lower income families.

A private, charitable network of emergency food providers (about 60,000 food banks and food pantries today) began in the late 1970s largely in response to a declining economy as well as cuts in a number of federal benefit programs (as noted earlier, this is also the period when America's income gaps began to widen leading to growing inequality). Keep in mind that these forms of assistance—both public and private—never provided enough resources to keep all eligible households comfortably food secure. Ever since their founding, and even during periods of genuine bipartisanship (Senators George McGovern (D) and Robert Dole (R) often worked together on behalf of these programs—see essay on McGovern), conservative political forces in and out of Congress kept up a barrage of opposition that prevented federal nutrition programs from fully meeting their goals. These reactionary forces were met in kind with a highly competent and vigilant cadre of advocates who, in many cases, devoted their careers to protecting and enhancing the programs that conservatives vehemently fought to curtail or even terminate.

While the public and private food programs that were so carefully nurtured and protected performed stalwart service in keeping widespread hunger from the nation's door (the current food insecurity levels would be much worse without them), we cannot say they fully answered the call to justice. The reasons I would posit are twofold. First, our understanding of the food system grew ever larger and more sophisticated as time went on. Food's interrelationship between such things as health, climate, workers, land, animals, culture, and economic development, to just name a few large pieces of the food system puzzle, became increasingly evident. While the vast array of public and private food programs has done an admirable job of providing the necessary calories to those whose financial circumstances made them food insecure, they do not, with limited exceptions (WIC and School Meals are more nutrition conscious) take into account the multiple connections to other food system sectors.

The second limitation speaks to the very nature of justice itself. Though food programs do target the disadvantaged, they fall far short of digging down into the roots of injustice that is ultimately necessary to eliminate the underlying causes of food insecurity. Much food assistance, especially in the private sector (e.g., food banks), is by design charitable. Its purpose is to alleviate the immediate conditions in a person's life that place them at risk of hunger, i.e., by giving them food. Public programs provide a much higher level of regularity and, generally, longer duration of food provisions than do private measures, but do not in and of themselves speak to the yawning income, wealth, education, and health gaps (to name a few) that define today's injustices.

Of course, none of this is to say that substantial paths to a just food system haven't been forged by food advocates and activists of all stripes. Over the course of decades, people from small towns and farms to large cities and Washington, DC have not just pushed back against food injustices, they have created meaningful and sustainable alternatives. The essays that follow chronicle those places, people, and actions that have opened new avenues in an expanded conceptualization of food justice that includes the environment, animals, health, food access, democratic participation, and racial equality. By extension, they also have unlocked doors into an area I haven't fully developed in my introductory analysis so far, namely the concept of community. The lack of human intimacy and social connection within our food system—we don't know who produces our food; food processing, manufacturing, and distribution are largely mysteries to us; we are nothing but consumers in the food industry's eyes—keep most of us in the dark. Fortunately, thousands of projects that model a way to a more community-oriented food system and a just society have evolved.

The lack of intimacy and connection may sound like an endearing but unnecessary feature of our lives in a food system that many think of as nothing but a series of economic transactions, producing profits for many and misery for many more. Sure, we'd all love to have more intimacy in our daily interactions, but in comparison, say, to the severity of hunger or the epidemic of diet-related diseases, perhaps it should be relegated to a much lower priority. But try living without intimacy for a long time at a personal level, then experience every day the cold efficiency of harshly lit, big box stores; extend those realities to all aspects of our commercial lives and before too long, pieces of our humanity slough away.

Take an experience that most of us have on a fairly regular basis—eating in a restaurant. In a parting newspaper column, the now former *New York Times* restaurant reviewer of twelve years, Pete Wells, bemoaned the loss of human connection that he always regarded as an essential part of the eating out experience. "From the moment we walked in [to a restaurant]" Wells (2024) noted,

> we talked with hosts, bartenders, captains, runners and bussers. Being served in a restaurant wasn't passive. We had to participate ... Many of the little routines of dining that we used to handle by talking to a person now happen on a screen ... Restaurants are turning into vending machines with chairs ... We've lost so many of the personal exchanges we used to have in restaurants.

The rest of our food system mirrors Wells's hundreds of restaurant engagements writ large. What we see in my stories to come are consequences of our communities' disconnection (and sometimes disintegration), not only with food but also within multiple sectors of society. The damage will be visible, but the sound of hammers and saws making the necessary repairs will create a din over which only optimism and cooperation can be heard.

The Divides Persist

To bridge certain societal and cultural divides, even when it comes to something as modest in scope as food, it helps to plunge back into the history of the nation's larger divides for both historical and cultural context, as well as to find a measure of hope. It's striking, for instance, to look back at Abraham Lincoln's second inaugural address which, near the end of the nation's greatest collective bloodletting and catastrophic breach, called for a reunification of the nation "with malice toward none; with charity for all; with firmness in the right." In today's political climate, it's nearly impossible to imagine finding a diverse audience willing to take such a message to heart.

Returning to Putnam's *Upswing*, we can see a pattern of social and cultural divides that, chronologically speaking, mirror the same timeframes of economic equality and inequality. In spite of Lincoln's magnanimous gesture, followed by a brief healing hiatus after the Civil War known as Reconstruction, racism—its governance and enforcement structures temporarily dismantled, but its virulence inside the human bloodstream as robust as ever—would be codified for 100 years across the Jim Crow South. In a slightly less overt and offensive form, it would find itself woven into the conversation of polite company across the nation with such concepts as "social Darwinism" and "survival of the fittest," in other words, a tacit acceptance of the false presumptions of the inferiority of the Black race. Such pseudo-science would also be applied to the various waves of European immigrants landing on America's shores from the late nineteenth into the early twentieth centuries. It would find contemporary expression in the false claims and accusations leveled against today's migrants, often fleeing violence, repression, and abysmal poverty. Nothing denies and severs humanity from itself—nor evokes more vitriolic forms of hate—like race, ethnicity, and nationality.

But against this negative backdrop a more positive and progressive notion would reveal itself in policy and prose. Instead of actions and words that divided, from the 1920s into the 1960s, political leaders like Franklin Delano Roosevelt (FDR), Henry Wallace (first FDR's Agriculture Secretary and later his vice president), and, yes, even Herbert Hoover, talked of "association," "cooperation," "compromise," and "unity." Putnam points out that one term, "common man," became "a powerful symbol of national solidarity, social equality, and communitarianism" in the 1940s (Putnam, 2020). Hoover, whose conservative principles earned him a respectable share of the blame for the Great Depression, surprisingly penned the book *American Individualism* where he argued that "laissez-faire was irresponsible, and that individualism without equal opportunity was repressive ... [and that individualism] must combine personal initiative with a deep spiritual commitment to ... public service and the importance of cooperation" (Putnam, 2020).

Of course, there's nothing like a take-no-prisoners economic depression followed by a horrific world war to force people to choose between standing together or dying alone. But as the crises that spawned a high degree of national solidarity faded, the ensuing economic prosperity of the post-war 1940s and 1950s continued to be buoyed by both an optimistic faith in the American project and a collectivist sentiment that placed the importance of "we" over "I." Americans would consistently invoke the "American Dream," first coined in 1931 by James Truslow Adams, who described the concept as "not a dream of motor cars and high wages merely, but a dream of social order in which [all people] attain ... the stature of what they are capable ... regardless of the fortuitous circumstances of their birth" (Putnam, 2020). The American Dream would reach its moral and oratorical zenith in Martin Luther King, Jr.'s "I Have a Dream" speech in 1963 before the term would be consumed by the giant maw of Madison Avenue materialism.

The bottom line of my exceedingly brief survey of 100 years of American history and culture is that realism/division/racism/inequality (1870s to 1920s) would trump the idealism/unity/shared pursuit of a common purpose articulated by Lincoln. The obstacles of cynicism, individualism, and greed that followed the Reconstruction era would lose their potency as a more optimistic and communitarian sensibility would take hold in the 1920s and reach its peak in the 1960s.

But by the late 1970s, the pendulum was again swinging the other way. Starting with the viciousness of McCarthyism in the 1950s to the generation-wrenching Vietnam War of the 1960s and 1970s, Putnam documents the beginning of a period that witnessed the rise of individualism over community, symbolized in one example by the declining use of the pronoun "we" in favor of "I." This is a period that continues to this day, marked by a profound cultural shift whose intellectual seeds were planted by Ayn Rand's *Atlas Shrugged* (1957; second only to the Bible as the most read book of the twentieth century; she is quoted as saying, "Nobody has ever given a reason why man should be his brother's keeper") and continues into our contemporary, allegedly self-made billionaire and tech men period (fittingly, one of the most notable products they gave us was the "selfie"). It is unlikely you'll find another class of men who lived so in defiance of Emerson's admonition that "the man of genius apprises us not of his wealth but of the commonwealth."

It should be acknowledged that the embrace of individualism at the expense of community is not a trait unique to conservative politicians and hell-for-leather entrepreneurs. Since the 1970s more people of all persuasions have turned away from "responsibility"—as in civic responsibility, family responsibility, moral responsibility—and toward individual "rights" and "identity." Here, the experience is one of dilution of a larger set of principles, such as voting rights, toward an ever-expanding list of vaguely defined individual rights. As Putnam sees it, we now talk about the "rights of the unborn," "gun rights," and "white rights." In effect, responsibility has been decoupled from rights, whereas they used to walk hand-in-hand, as in "with rights come responsibilities." Today, no one who does not exercise their right to vote is ever held accountable, but if anyone allegedly infringes upon my property rights, attempts to restrict my gun rights, or has an abortion, accusations and lawsuits (or worse) will fly.

In similar fashion, "identity" has become a fast-growing concept in America's twenty-first century lexicon. But it has moved away from its use in the context of "we" (as in "we Americans") and much more within the confines of "I" (as in "I am gay"). In one survey, the use of "identity" soared from 1970 to 2010, but fewer than 3 percent of the word's uses involved reflections of collective or cultural identity such as "Black identity" or "gender identity." They were of a largely personal or individual identity.

In today's world, where so much of our vocabulary is drawn from the narcissistic palette of social media, it takes no small amount of determination to espouse a common good or public purpose. I sit at my desk writing this one week before the 2024 US presidential election. I'm astonished by how little I've heard throughout the campaign that is about "we" or offers a plan of cooperation or a unified approach to problem solving. The existential challenges of the day, like climate change demand deep collaboration, but the cultural moment we live in doesn't allow us to get beyond "me-centered" messages and issues like the current price of a gallon of milk or gas (data show these concerns linger in consumers' minds long after the actual prices have dropped to their lower levels). With one-half of the nation, more or less, in thrall to a man who is likely the most narcissistic public figure to walk the face of the planet since the Second World War, it is not clear when America's flight plan will once again, like it did after the First World War, find its path to more elevated heights and a common course. Do I dare find solace and a teaspoon of hope in the lyrics of the Grateful Dead, who in their song "Touch of Gray" the lyrics made a sudden shift from "I will survive," repeated over and over until the last stanza when it becomes "We will survive."

A Chance to Mend

The need to find bridges across our nation's great divides is why I turn to food and the stories you are about to read. Over the length and breadth of my fifty-five-year-long career in community organizing, development, and food justice, three essential elements of effective social and community change stand out: (1) imagination; (2) a clear focus on defined needs and responses; and (3) leadership that successfully conveys the importance of "we" over "I." Starting with we/I, a community or nation divided—with strongly competing visions, yawning economic and social gaps, violent resistance to new ideas, people, and approaches—is not a place that will have the confidence or capacity to close the divide(s) nor make strides in eliminating injustice(s). Therefore, imposing a "we" framework on the task is necessary, and it becomes the job of the leader(s) to do just that, whether through great ideas, inspiring leadership, or diligent, persistent, and competent work.[2] To that end, true justice, in the sense that Rawls defines it in his original principles, needs to be well articulated, not expressed in stilted academic prose nor in an esoteric code that's only understood by small numbers of insiders, but in a re-envisioned manner that moves the hearts and minds of the most people.

Within a food system context, one could apply the "veil of ignorance" to a community setting, for instance, to assemble the

---

[2]Throughout this leadership discussion I will use a single person leadership approach for ease of discussion, recognizing full well that more groups and organizations are leaning toward co-leadership models.

building blocks of food justice. Starting with the survival imperatives of healthy food and the natural resources required to produce it, a simple call for justice should extend its reach to the larger environment (e.g., global warming and climate change), and on to the humane treatment of animals. Calling on the rights framework of Rawls's first principle, as well as the subsection of the second principle—*attached to offices and positions open to all under conditions of fair equality of opportunity*—one can easily imagine those operating under a veil of ignorance to favor democratic citizen engagement—food sovereignty and food democracy as it were—in all facets of food system decision-making. Remember, those working under the veil are not beholden to market forces, special interests, identity, or any notion that wealth should be equated with power and privilege. Hence, they are likely to be moved by the human urge to participate in things (e.g., food) that matter the most to them, and to remain un-swayed by a few domineering food corporations or a handful of controlling elected officials who may, unjustly, make exclusive claims to all decisions based on their unilateral ownership or so-called obligation to their shareholders.

Moving backward into defined needs and responses, I turn not to formal community food assessments or other analytical tools commonly taught in today's graduate schools, but to something more ordinary as prescribed by philosophers and poets. "The literature of the poor, the feelings of the child, the philosophy of the street," Emerson tells us, "are the topics of the time … Give me insight into today, and you may have the antique and future worlds" (1957). Sit quietly and attentively with the injustices you see, and you will soon see their past and their prognosis. This is not to say that you don't keep your toolbox of analytical instruments nearby, but don't open it until you are certain which tool to reach for and how it will sharpen your insight. Your job is not to create new abstractions and theories, but to remove as much distance between yourself and the object of your interest as possible, and to embrace and interpret the poet William Carlos Williams's teaching, "No ideas but in things!" The thing, not the theory is the proper subject of inquiry—the people, places, and actions that make up your food system. Becoming thoroughly acquainted with those things are the building blocks of the inductive learning process.

As I've gone to and fro across a lifetime of community and national food work, I've kept a sharp eye open for analytical tools and the latest methods and theories that suggest promising directions. My naive hope as a practitioner had always been to find some modern miracle of social engineering that could be scaled up or down according to the size and circumstances of the problem, and further adjusted for the requisite cultural competencies to fit any given place and people. While so-called "best practices" and promising models abound, I've found no substitute for a small number of passionate and committed people, possessed of fiery imaginations, as the single most powerful force for change. After reading the French cellular geneticist turned wandering Buddhist monk and humanitarian, Matthieu Ricard, my own wanderings and wonderings as a food activist were confirmed by his statement, "All change is begun by a few people aware of the need to strive for a better world. They have the inner conviction that they can make their wishes and dreams come true" (Ricard, 2023). And to qualify the good monk's words, I might underscore "change" and "aware of the need to strive for a better world" to distinguish those who put the needs of lesser advantaged people ahead of themselves from those entrepreneurial-types, often canonized in the media, whose first priority is making billions for themselves and an elite group of followers.

Lastly, to address the first of my three essential elements for change, namely imagination, those leaders—that pioneering and inspired class of change agents—are powered by imaginations that view problems in the context of larger systems; this wider scope enables them to create new connections and solutions. I address this topic more directly in a piece in this book titled "The Poetry of Community Food Assessments" where I argue for a more open-minded and subjective approach to community work. I draw on the sense and sensibility of poetry as a metaphor for direct engagement with experiences that can be seen and understood subjectively from many different angles. That immersion in experience is as vital to all food system practitioners as it is to the poet. As the poet Derek Walcott said, "To change your language, you must change your life."

Turning to poems and poetry should not imply some form of navel gazing or idealistic flights of fancy—though such ways of seeing and living have their purpose—but as ways of sharpening our senses and intellects to realities often obscured by formalistic, data-laden research methods. As the sociologist C. Wright Mills said in *The Sociological Imagination*, "It has been forgotten that social observation requires high skill and acute sensibility; that discovery often occurs precisely when an imaginative mind sets itself down in the middle of social realities" (Mills, 1959).

My Purpose

In the same fashion that the people I write about have beaten an imaginative path to important alterations in their food systems, they have graciously granted me permission to tarry awhile among them. With my notebook and audio recorder in hand, I have inserted myself into the work of others over the past twenty years to glean a treasure trove of insights. My stated purpose has been twofold: gather enough information to assemble a theory of food system change, and give others the space they need to tell their story. To those ends, they have shown remarkable forbearance for my sometimes, ignorant questions, obtuseness, and occasional misstatements that my hastiness produced. Their indulgence is deeply appreciated.

Two more points should be made clear before we begin. The first is that it's not my intention to offer detailed prescriptions for good leadership, collaboration strategies, community development methods, and other more granular techniques that any practitioner or student would normally find useful. I have done much of that elsewhere (see *Stand Together or Starve Alone*), and instead wish to maintain the focus on the people, places, and actions highlighted in the following essays. By way of example and illustration, they will provide valuable instruction to anyone who sees themselves playing a role—no matter how large or small—in food justice work. To provide a minimal enhancement, I have written a short preface to each essay to suggest certain themes for particular consideration.

Secondly, I am generally known by others, as well as to myself, as an older white male who has spent his entire adult life working on food issues, primarily those that affect people of color, communities of color, and people and places with limited resources. My position on injustice/justice is largely influenced by that work. My chosen vehicle has generally been non-profit organizations that serve the same constituencies that are the primary object of my concern and engagement. Nevertheless, I grew up in privileged social and economic circumstances that positioned me nicely and easily to, among other opportunities, attend an excellent college. That experience, in concert with all the advantages a forward-looking, well-educated, and affluent family can bestow upon a young person, gave me the credentials and advantages one needs to pursue a successful life, both personally and professionally. I am grateful for all that, yet I acknowledge that it will always affect how I view the world, which in turn, no matter how immersed I may be in different cultures and communities, will always influence my words, analysis, and behavior.

A Word About the Essays

The essays that follow are a selection of blog posts drawn from markwinne.com dating back to 2010. The op-ed piece for the *Washington Post* appeared in November 2007, and a speech given to the American Community Garden Association is reprinted from a 2010 transcript. Of course, there are many more essays available from where these come from, but for purposes of inclusion in this book they have been selected for their diversity of subject matter, geography, and racial and ethnic associations. Additionally, the book's themes of social justice, the qualities of leadership, and the role of imagination run through these essays and should be considered for the way they practically illustrate the points made in the Introduction. However, it should not be assumed that the essays are a direct or absolute expression of those themes but merely an application of them within the larger context of people, places, and actions, which is how I have chosen to organize the essays.

Place: From the physical terrain to the demographics to the cultural context, it's necessary to understand the unique characteristics that shape any particular community, jurisdiction, or region. Those characteristics and the dynamic interaction between them not only tell you what this place is, it can tell you what it can become. With respect to understanding food systems, there are elements that are common to all communities as well as ones that are idiosyncratic or even original to specific places. Most places have both. But what is clear is that the concept of a food system applies to all places, big or small, rural or urban, and that nearly all communities across the country have developed robust projects, businesses, and initiatives that are viable alternatives to the dominant, industrial food system. I explore these points and relationships more fully in my book *Food Town USA* (Winne, 2019). The places highlighted by this book's essays offer a reasonable representation of community food systems from around the country.

People: The story of the food movement and its role in promoting social justice cannot be divorced from the people who made it happen, whether at a high profile, national level or more modestly at the community level. My experience working in communities made me an adherent of Ralph Waldo Emerson's statement that "There is no history, only biography." While that assertion can certainly be judged an over-simplification given the infinite complexities and broad context of any social movement, one person, in one place, taking a stand for an idea they believe in, is often a necessary starting point and a key ingredient, if not a prerequisite, for change. Even when their presence and profile are diluted as others swarm to the cause, there are key individuals who remain the germ from which many shoots sprout.

Action: While not independent of people or places, the actions that take place within a food system tend to draw their energy from a wider arena of ideas. A new idea may be initially situated in a particular place or be the spark of one person or a small group, but its dissemination nationwide takes on a life of its own. So does its inevitable critique or assessment, which will lead to improvements, alterations, or even dismissal as it is tested and adapted in multiple places. Actions should always be subject to critique and review—that makes them stronger and better able to serve targeted as well as wider communities—and, therefore, transparency and robust debate is part of their evolution. Action examples contained within these essays, like the people and place essays, are not meant to be an exhaustive offering of the vast list of the common food system actions of the last twenty years. They do tend, however, to look closely at how ideas have emerged, evolved, and been applied, particularly at certain points in time.

Lastly, these essays were written based on the circumstances, information, and people that were available at the time the story was researched and written. If new information has come to light that might materially affect our understanding and assessment of the events and underlying themes, I have included them as "Updates" at the end of the essay. Otherwise, each essay stands on its own merit, as it was reported, unaltered, as of the date after the title.

PART ONE

Places

CHAPTER ONE

Great Falls, Great Food, Great Gaps: The Tale of Paterson and Ridgewood

May, 2023

Here I've taken a side-by-side look at urban/suburban inequality through both a larger socioeconomic and a local food lens. Like many places, there is bad news and good news; systemic injustices and extraordinary acts of do-it-yourself activism; public sector ineptitude and displays of public sector courage and innovation. All of this is set against a notable poetic and cultural backdrop that is surrounded by vast stores of wealth. This piece was the first of a two-part series, the second part devoted primarily to Ridgewood, NJ can be found at markwinne.com. Biggest surprise: Beauty matters.

How do I tell an accurate story about places that are embedded in my subjectivity? On the surface it's a food story because that's nearly all I know, but it's also a personal story rooted in the memory of my agitated youth. Decades of experience and reflections have sharpened its edges. Clouds of data have settled like stardust across the plain of my consciousness giving objectivity a stronger foothold.

Yet the affluent suburb of Ridgewood, New Jersey, my hometown, and its rough and ready neighboring city, Paterson, occupy a large compartment of my soul where the two places remain divided by a concrete Jersey barrier.

The story begins in the 1950s with two buses—one is brown and the other is yellow. The brown one carried business men from Ridgewood to the New York City Port Authority Bus Terminal, where they would fan out across midtown to their respective corporate office buildings. The yellow bus transported women from Paterson—about seven miles away—to my town's tony neighborhoods where they would make their way to the private homes of residents to clean, cook, and care for their children. My house was one of them. The women were known as "cleaning ladies," they were Black, and my siblings and me called them by their first names even though they were often older than our mother.

Both buses motored up and down Monroe Street, the same route I used to walk or bike to school. Late in the afternoon, as I made my way home, the brown bus would sometimes pass the yellow bus as each was returning riders to their respective homes. Occasionally, I noticed the Black women turn their heads to look at the white men whose faces were buried in their evening newspaper. I wondered what these women thought, what Paterson was like, and who, if anyone, cared for them. I knew about the white men. One of them was my father and others were fathers of my friends. The cleaning ladies, who we politely referred to as Negroes, or sometimes "colored," only traveled fifteen minutes by bus, but for a ten-year-old Ridgewood boy, Paterson was as remote and mysterious as Mars.

When you don't know stuff, you tend to make it up, and what we made up about a place as dark and distant as Paterson was often fueled by racism and white privilege. In that sense, the things you don't know, or know incorrectly, also become the source of your fear. We saw Paterson as Black, dangerous, and poor. It was the place you did not take your date on Saturday night. It was where Rubin "Hurricane" Carter, a contender for the middleweight boxing crown, was falsely accused of murder in 1966, convicted, imprisoned, later spotlighted by Bob Dylan, and not released until 1985. It was the site of civil disturbances in 1968 following Rev. Martin Luther King, Jr.'s assassination. It was a place where police corruption and incompetence exceeded even New Jersey's legendary standards of skulduggery. (And it is, unfortunately, still such a place: the New Jersey attorney general took control of the Paterson police department this March, due to its inability to manage itself, including police killings of Black men.)

In an effort to gain some clarity over these dissembling memories, I embarked on a modest pilgrimage to Ridgewood and Paterson to look at each place afresh, and as I am wont to do, I did it through a food lens. Food gives me a place to pivot from, a solid and necessary footing from where I can interpret a city's broader social and economic dimensions, perhaps ones that would afford me more accurate views into my discontent. But the food lens was not just a vocational choice, it was also because the region's poetic godfather, William Carlos Williams and his epic twentieth-century poem "Paterson" admonished, "Say it! No ideas but in things." To capture the truth, in other words, I had to let my ideas grow out of the reality and immediacy of people, their deeds, and nature. Those are the things that matter, and I can think of no better thing than food.

To begin, a community's food system has much to do with its social and economic conditions, and since numbers are also things, or at least representative of other things, here's an abbreviated side-by-side comparison of Ridgewood and Paterson (all figures are for 2021).

Table 1.1 Demographic comparison of Ridgewood and Paterson

	Ridgewood	Paterson
Population	26,202	157,794
Median household income ($)	194,256	48,450
Persons without health insurance. (%)	2.9	20.9
Average life expectancy (years)	86	74
Poverty rate (%)	2.6	25.1
Bachelor's degree or higher (%)	78.3	12.5
Black or African-American (%)	1.2	24.7
Hispanic or Latino (%)	8.7	62.6

(Source: US Census. Population Estimates, July 1, 1922 (V2822))

These are the things that tell a tale of two cities. Ridgewood and Paterson are geographically close, but the socioeconomic differences are achingly far apart. To place Paterson in a larger metro New York context, Mary Celis, president and CEO of the Passaic County United Way put it this way, "Paterson is only nineteen miles from Wall Street."

Imbalances like these translate into long-term consequences for children. Take education, for instance. Despite hundreds of millions of dollars of investment by the State of New Jersey over the past two decades, Paterson Public Schools—which educate nearly 25,000 students in more than forty school buildings, seventeen of which are over 100 years old—remain in desperate need of new facilities and extensive repairs (northjersey.com). Without the tax base to adequately support its physical infrastructure, to say nothing of ongoing operations, the Paterson school system must rely on mostly inadequate aid from the New Jersey legislature whose often unsympathetic suburban members look askance at urban needs.

> ... *poor, the invisible, thrashing, breeding, debased city*
> "Paterson" by William Carlos Williams

Never could such conditions be imagined for Ridgewood schools. My parents deliberately moved there in the early 1950s because even then the schools had a reputation for being among the finest in the state. Later, new residents would mortgage themselves to the hilt for the privilege of settling themselves anywhere within the village's boundaries so that their little Marks and Susies could one day claim a diploma from Ridgewood High School. Of course, the property taxes required to maintain an exceptional educational standard would suck the marrow from your bones. A classmate of mine and former mayor of Ridgewood is reputed to have said that residents will never flinch from raising taxes in order to support the schools—that, effectively, the sky's the limit. So steep is the "membership dues" that, as the tale goes, the lawn signs congratulating Mark and Susie for graduating from Ridgewood High in June are soon replaced by for-sale signs in July.

> *Paterson lies in the valley under the Passaic Falls ...*
> *In a recoil of spray and rainbow mists ...*
> "Paterson"

Given that Paterson was envisioned by Alexander Hamilton in 1792 as America's first industrial center, there is more than a little irony in the city's struggling financial condition today. Building off the Passaic River and its Great Falls potential for energy generation, a system of channels was constructed to power textile mills and later the manufacturing of locomotives and airplane engines. Hamilton led the founding of the Society for Establishing Useful Manufactures (S.U.M.), New Jersey's first corporation, to oversee what became a juggernaut of creation, technology, and industrial output.

When the demand for all that productive might declined after the Second World War, so did the surrounding economy. Today, the Great Falls, a still functioning hydroelectric plant, and the Paterson Museum are joined loosely around the Paterson Great Falls National Historical Park, which is now part of the National Park System. Nearby, you will find recently revitalized Hinchliffe Field, one of only two remaining Negro League baseball stadiums in the country. It stands as a testament to the national shame of segregation and the resilience of Black athletes. The reactivated stadium is also accompanied by the construction of seventy-five units of affordable senior housing, both projects instigated by Paterson's Mayor Andre Sayegh.

As with similar efforts I've seen in other cities, where a well-intentioned economic comeback is underway, the focus is often on burnishing one gem while ignoring the setting. The Falls and the adjoining viewing areas created by the Park Service are one of the more spectacular natural sites in the mid-Atlantic region. And if you take the time to absorb the totality of US history compressed into this one small area, most people would not fail to be impressed. Unfortunately, the surrounding neighborhoods are in disrepair and probably on some city list for renovation. The signage, roadways, and parking in and around the historic site will leave the visitor hopelessly bewildered (I swear, Siri told me, "Sorry pal, you're on your own!"). The general maintenance and appearance of the area are such that you could imagine the Paterson Sanitation Department, some private museum board of directors, and the Park Service arguing over whose job it is to pick up the trash, fix the broken fences, or provide a minimum of landscape services. On the day I visited, the main roadway into the historic area was closed while emergency construction crews repaired an aging street that appeared to retain vestiges of Hamilton's wagon ruts.

In spite of all this, it's worth a visit!

Against this backdrop, it's not surprising that food has become both an opportunity and a challenge. Andre Sayegh—the city's youthful and visionary second-term mayor—is using food as a part of the city's comeback plan. I was admittedly delighted to see Paterson's home page tagline read "Great Falls, Great Food, Great Future!" No argument from me about the Falls; the city's multi-ethnic restaurant scene (there are seventy-two nationalities represented among city residents) may one day put Paterson on some kind of regional food map; as to the future, well, time will tell.

Consistent with his aspirations, the mayor, a lifelong resident of Paterson with a Jimmy Fallon-like personality, did a video of a five-restaurant food crawl with northjersey.com's food editor, Esther Davidowitz (2022). Together, they noshed their way down Palestinian Way, an honorary street name selected to recognize the city's Palestinian population, the second largest in the US. To call the blocks along Palestinian Way a food Mecca is more than an obvious pun—the large number of halal food outlets and mosques speak to the depth and diversity of Paterson's Arab community—it is also a rich and rewarding cultural immersion.

Having had lunch at Al-Basha, one of the restaurants on their crawl, I can attest to how delicious the cuisine is. In their video, Sayegh and Davidowitz sampled hummus, compared the restaurants various baba ganoush dishes, waxed enthusiastic over an okra and meat creation served over rice, and had a cute argument about the correct shape of falafels. What stood out for me about the piece were two things: that a city mayor would celebrate his community's cuisine with so much articulate gusto, and that one of the region's major media outlets would raise up restaurants in a tattered city that would not be seen as a dining-out destination by its generally prosperous viewers (the broadcast's opening line captured that ambivalence: "Been to Paterson lately? Ever?"). In a not-unrelated note, Mayor Sayegh also understands the connection between calories in and calories out. One of his quality-of-life initiatives is to have active outdoor recreation space no more than a half-mile from any residential dwelling—no small task in a city as densely built as Paterson.

But the big food challenge is not where to eat out, it's food insecurity—affordability, access, and dietary health. Paterson has a large low-income population, virtually nothing of economic substance to anchor its tax base, and not enough financial fuel to rev up its economic growth engines. Capturing as much economic benefit from food—normal household consumption, restaurants, and various food chain activities—is an obvious default position for a resource-poor place. But until the time when a rising economy can lift all ships, people must be fed, and to do that well in Paterson requires a steep climb up a mountain of food injustices.

In 2021, the New Jersey Department of Economic Development conducted a statewide food desert and access study. Using the USDA standard definitions, the study identified fifty areas around the state—urban, suburban, and rural—as food deserts and then ranked them as to their comparative "desertification." Paterson's southside was the thirteenth worst while its northside came in at number 15 (New Jersey Development Authority, 2022).

The ironic accompaniment to a food desert is a food swamp—an oversaturation of fast-food places and low-nutritious food outlets of which Paterson is awash. Filling in the food landscape, and in response to high levels of food insecurity, Paterson is also home to five large food pantries, each receiving over $500,000 a year through Emergency and Shelter funding, according to Mary Celis of United Way of Passaic County, which sponsors the Passaic County Food Policy Council (Passaic County Food Policy Council, 2025).

Food studies like New Jersey's and the tabulations of a city's other food outlets can tell you a lot about a food environment, but they don't reflect how people living in those places cope with a multitude of realities that an anti-poor marketplace imposes on them. To get a better sense of that, I had lunch with Mary and six of her Food Policy Council members at Al-Basha's.

Clearly, themes of underinvestment/disinvestment and their impacts on Paterson's food system were strongly shared by everyone. "Good food is not available in Paterson," was the conclusion reached by Deacon Willie Davis, one of the city's leading urban agriculturalists. This was echoed by others including Kimmeshia Rogers-Jones, a social worker and long-time community activist who sees the small grocery stores that remain in the city and those just beyond its borders as predators who take advantage of

Paterson's BIPOC community. "They know we're coming because we have no choice, which is why they have low-quality food. Go to a Shop-Rite [a regional supermarket chain] in Fair Lawn, Wayne, or Paramus [higher income, nearby towns] and the quality is much more improved." She also expressed her frustration with local food insecurity: "It's mind-boggling to be in a rich country when we have so many hungry people in Paterson."

Shana Manradge, a food entrepreneur and founder of A Better Market, said, "We [BIPOC residents] go to places where bad food is because 'they' know we'll buy it! What's affordable to us is not healthy and causes diseases—that's the inequity!" The relation between the low quality of available and affordable food, and what's healthy was underscored by Darryl Jackson, a teacher and political activist. A number of years ago, Darryl adopted veganism as his primary diet in reaction to the unhealthy food that filled his neighborhood. "I realized how addicted I had become to the sugars and salt around me. I realized how my body was affected by the food available in my community." While he likes to make it clear he's "not militant" about his choice to be vegan—"I'll eat whatever in the company of others"—he feels passionately that there's a strong relationship between Paterson's low-quality food, the residents' health, and their low levels of activism. "Not enough people act against these injustices because their food undermines their vitality [including] not knowing how to grow their food."

The more macro aggressions of society's injustices were also highlighted. Steve Kehayes from Habitat for Humanity reiterated that "access to safe and affordable food and housing are human rights," ones that the group felt were not fulfilled in Paterson. Lisa Martin from City Green, a statewide gardening organization, pointed out that there's a need for a living wage to be paid to everyone. As the leader of the Passaic County United Way, Mary Celis confronts the depth and breadth of the region's inequalities and their consequences every day. She bemoaned the absence of fair tax policies that would progressively tax and equitably distribute wealth and income. "The nation's COVID allotments and waivers ended which reduced the expanded Child Tax Credit and SNAP benefits and is impacting access to Medicaid. These policy changes are having adverse effects on people in Passaic County, and they are issues that the Food Policy Council cares dearly about," she said.

Beauty is a defiance of authority.
"Paterson"

Much to my surprise, the subject of nature's beauty came up as something that was lacking in Paterson. Maybe it was because I grew up under the canopy of Ridgewood's well-tended shade trees and walked through dappled light my whole young life that I took nature's soothing and salutary effects for granted. To lie in the grass and gaze up at the leafy majesty of my lot's massive oaks was a gift I naturally assumed was available to all. I guess that's why I was a little shocked when Kimmeshia said, "Beauty isn't just a suburban thing. We should have it here too! We need more gardens like Deacon Davis's in the 4th Ward. It's so beautiful!" Lisa Martin added with just a hint of irony, "After all, this is the Garden State!"

And in that spirit, knowing that waiting for an under-resourced city to intervene was like waiting for Godot, these citizens are cooking up their own solutions. I made my way on a cool day in late April to the Green Acre Community Garden at 12th and Rosa Parks Avenue. That's where I found Deacon Davis presiding over an outdoor "chapel" of raised vegetable beds, a greenhouse, and an array of fruit trees that he's been developing and tending since 2014. Lettuce, early collards, and onions were poking their heads above the soil and soon would be joined by a steady flow of fresh, summer vegetables. At the age of seventy-two, Deacon Davis is as fit as spring fiddlehead. He works circles around those who are half his age so that he and his volunteers can give away thousands of pounds of fresh produce to the people of the 4th Ward. "My agenda is for the people, not for profit," he said.

The garden, which is one of the more attractive urban gardens I've seen anywhere, has numerous partners including Habitat for Humanity, City Green, and the United Way. But clearly it is Deacon Davis's diligent and nurturing presence that bathes a harsh, urban environment with beauty. He comes from a family of Black North Carolina sharecroppers who taught him how to farm, but, like millions of other Black farmers, was victimized by that brutal and racist form of agriculture. "I grew up in a house with no running water or electricity," he tells me. "One night before I went to sleep, I placed a bucket of water next to my bed. When I woke that morning, it was frozen." Emerging from these circumstances remarkably unembittered, he said "I also learned a lot of patience." As I stood with him and Mary Celis taking in the abundance of his horticultural achievements, a steady stream of residents walked by calling out, "Hi, Deacon Davis," and "How are you, Deacon Davis?" Clearly, the Deacon is a beacon.

Shana Manradge is another member of the Food Policy Council who's taking matters into her own hands. Frustrated by the distance she must drive from her home to buy healthy food, she decided to go into the retail food business in a most unusual way. When she swings her garage door open in the driveway of her modest house, you'll find grocery shelves and refrigerators filled with food instead of a Subaru. Packed with produce and chicken from Black-owned farms in South Jersey (K&J Organic Farm and Smith Poultry) and a variety of nonperishable food items from local food entrepreneurs, Shana started "A Better Market," which currently serves sixty households a week at prices that beat those of area supermarket chains (A Better Market, 2025). One of Shana's specialties is a bag that contains $40 of fresh produce that she sells for $25. "People in Paterson have to go too far to find real food. I want to make it available right here!"

While Shana pays herself a small salary, it doesn't cover the many hours required to pick up food, run the store, advertise, and conduct endless rounds of outreach. For all of these tasks she taps into a full reservoir of willing volunteers including a high school student who produces a weekly flyer, Deacon Davis who rounded up a free refrigerator unit, and countless friends and church members who lift crates, sort produce, and price goods. Her midterm goal is to find an affordable brick and mortar store so she can reach more people and also accept food stamps, a physical facility being a USDA requirement for SNAP certification.

The State of New Jersey is not indifferent to the injustices that befall places like Paterson. When compared to surrounding, mostly white suburbs like Ridgewood, Paterson exists under a system of food apartheid. In an attempt to rectify that condition, the New Jersey Economic Development Authority has committed $40 million to invest in the state's food desert communities. Mary Celis and her team put together a proposal for a portion of those funds for a Paterson project. (Just as this blog went to press, they received word that they will be awarded a $125,000 grant from the state that "will be used to develop a feasibility study for a supermarket, food retailer, or farmers market to be located within a mixed-use development site in Paterson.")

Paterson's problems are complex and deep, and the wealth and income gaps in North Jersey are wide and frustrating, especially when you see the region's islands of intense poverty surrounded by one of the heaviest concentrations of financial power in the world. People like Deacon Davis and Shana Manradge bootstrap their way from one bushel of produce to the next; the United Way dutifully assembles one funding proposal after another to secure money for badly needed projects; Mayor Sayegh cobbles together $100 million to renovate a former Negro League ballpark to restore some of the city's glory days. This is how it's done in crumbling places like Paterson—a combination of local heroes, persistent social service organizations, imperfect and at times ambivalent state governments, and an earnest elected official or two keep the boat afloat, but their efforts alone are never enough to beach it firmly on the shores of prosperity.

When I asked the food activists gathered at Al-Basha what their number one priority for action would be, they responded with near unanimity: Kids! Better schools for kids, better food in the schools for kids, a garden in every school, etc. "Would you feed this food to your children? That was the question I asked the board of health," Kimmeshia Rogers-Jones told the group, referring to the city's overall food environment. "To me, that's the only test that matters. I would prefer to shop in Paterson, but I can't serve that food to my family!"

As I was wondering why people like Deacon Davis, Shana, and Mary go to such lengths to secure food and rebuild a once beautiful city, I remembered a passage from James Baldwin's extraordinary essay, "Nobody Knows My Name" (1961). He cites the substandard conditions of segregated Southern Black schools and their abysmal educational results. As school integration proceeded in the face of white hatred and violence, Baldwin asks if "those Negro parents who spend their days trembling for their children" place them at such risk (some days their children return home covered in the spit of their white antagonists) out of some set of ideals? No, he answers himself, "They are doing it because they want the child to receive the education which will allow him to ... one day abolish the stifling environment in which they see, daily, so many children perish" (Baldwin, 1961).

I suspect that is why Paterson's people do what they do. They want their children to overcome the conditions that will, if not corrected, cut decades from their lives.

Update: The long arm of Paterson's zoning code finally caught up with Shana Manradge and A Better Market, determining that it violated too many regulations to ignore. But this only made Shana more determined to realize her dream of opening up a "brick and mortar" grocery story, which she did on August 24, 2024 on Rosa Parks Blvd. across from Deacon Davis's garden. She also plans to introduce a mobile grocery as adjunct to the store.

CHAPTER TWO

New Roots Community Farm: "This is the coolest place I've ever been!"

September, 2023

Working the land, getting your hands in the dirt, finding community in the shared enterprise of feeding yourself, neighbors, and those in need are emotionally laden values that have rippled through, indeed, inspired the food movement since the 1960s. But to hitch that physical and mental energy to the task of also rebuilding economically depressed communities raises the bar much higher on what had previously been a more limited form of agriculture. In this West Virginia community, we find visionary leadership, extraordinary teamwork, and a powerful form of social entrepreneurism set to the task of healing both people and place. Biggest surprise: Pies, Pints, and Pesto.

To come here originally as a volunteer was like stepping into a new world ... I don't want to just grow food for myself; I want to grow for my neighbor so they can see you don't have to settle for Walmart.
I'm on this planet to work with land.
–Staff comments from the New Roots Community Farm, Fayette County, West Virginia

The place, food, and land referenced above are the New Roots Community Farm, an 82-acre non-profit agricultural center whose fields unroll like a plush carpet across the Fayette County, West Virginia hills. The voices are some of the dozen or so young people in their twenties and thirties who dig, tend, and pick an intensively cultivated six-acre section of the site to sell, share, and deliver its produce to a surrounding community of local shoppers, senior citizens, school children, and a food bank. The occasion is a more or less spontaneous evening meal in the farm's barn, suggested by me and orchestrated by New Roots co-founder and director, Gabe Pena. The ingredients include several smoked chickens from a nearby farm; various vegetable dishes gleaned from the nearby field; wine, beer, and homemade ice cream. The topic of discussion, selected for both its physical and metaphysical layers, is "why are you here?"

Why was I here? Having spent a couple of days talking to people in and around Mingo County at West Virginia's southwest border with Kentucky, I was hoping to find a brighter sense of what the region's future might look like. Were there places—potential models—with similar demographics and challenges to Mingo that were reinventing themselves, unchained from coal and its legacies of poverty, ill-health, and drug addiction? Some tipsters I had encountered along the way sent me two hours east to Fayette County where I found people building a new economy and community out of the shell of the old.

Though Fayette's population of 41,000 is almost twice the size of Mingo's, that number, like Mingo's, is half of what it was in 1950 (although some recent growth has been reported). Otherwise, Fayette County has seen three coal mines close over the past few years, its poverty rate hovers a bit over 20 percent, and dietary health problems associated with residents' high obesity rates make the local health-care industry among the area's top three employers.

And like other rural counties, a severe case of political whiplash has shifted voters radically from the reliably blue end of the spectrum to the deep red. In Fayette County, for instance, the three county commissioner seats were held by Democrats as recently as 2015. Today, they are all Republicans.

Coming to Fayette from Texas in 2007, Gabe, now thirty-nine, didn't get into farming for any of the sentimental reasons that often drive some young people to plunge their hands into the soil. "Economic development is a passion of mine; in fact, I can get quite wonky about it," he tells me as he takes his car into a steep dive descending into the nearby New River Gorge, somehow straightening out one hairpin turn after another. "Food access is critical to our economy and one of the social determinants of health which are integral parts of economic development. Part of our impetus for developing New Roots was knowing that local food businesses can work hand-in-hand with our tourism industry as part of an economic diversification strategy," he says, taking his eyes off the road just a little longer than I'd like.

When we reach the gorge's bottom, I begin to see what he means. We are crossing the New River, which along with the cliffs rising 900 feet straight up on each side constitutes the striking natural features of what became the New River Gorge National Park and Preserve in 2020. It offers unparalleled whitewater rafting, hiking, and rock-climbing opportunities, which, along with more passive sightseeing uses, have attracted 1.7 million outdoor enthusiasts in less than four years (compare this to the estimated 20,000 tourists who come each year to Mingo County primarily for ATV trail riding).

Perhaps the Park's most dramatic feature happens to be manmade—the New River Gorge Bridge, the longest steel span bridge in the Western Hemisphere and third highest in the United States. Gabe told me that on the third weekend in October the bridge serves as a BASE jumping site (Bridge, Antennae, Span, and Earth) which sees hundreds of people hurling themselves off the bridge—parachutes attached—into the gorge below, a sport I don't see myself taking up anytime soon.

Gabe doesn't confine his activities to just being a community food project developer and policy wonk, he's also an active local food citizen. After working for the Fayette County planning office, he decided that local government needed younger people serving in decision-making roles, so he ran for the Fayetteville City Council and won. Taking me on a walking tour of downtown Fayetteville, Gabe makes his agenda crystal clear by pointing out the tweaks that would make the town more vital. "I want to facilitate 'small development,'" he tells me.

Pointing to one corner restaurant, he explains how the town wouldn't let it have an outdoor, sidewalk eating area that would bring more life to downtown. Similarly, they turned down a request for a food truck even though they've become ubiquitous elsewhere these days. Passing an abandoned building that had housed a microbrew restaurant, Gabe says the town wouldn't upgrade the sewer system, which would have allowed the pub to do on-site brewing. "We have an overabundance of a protectionist mentality that impedes innovative business projects," which is perhaps a wonky way of saying that the town doesn't yet have a robust sense of its own potential. Gabe is working on changing that.

Though unstated, the mutually beneficial connection between local food establishments and the New Roots Farm, only two miles from downtown Fayetteville, is certainly apparent. Pies and Pints is a downtown pizza and brew joint popular with the rafter and climbing crowd. One of New Roots young farmers tells me the restaurant hosts an annual "Pies, Pints, and Pesto" festival that consumes nearly all the farm's entire basil crop. Sure, Gabe and the New Roots board of directors love the revenue stream generated by its farm to restaurant sales, but the bigger vision is what excites them. What would the economic impact on the region be if tourist demand drove restaurant business, which drove demand for local produce, which drove the growth in the number of new farms across the county and adjoining counties? And we're not just talking about an outdoor recreationist-fueled, pesto-topped pizza feeding frenzy. Extend that local vision to institutional sales like schools and hospitals, connect the $800 million of federal food assistance (e.g., SNAP, school meal programs) spending in West Virginia every year to local food production, and consider large grants to food banks that could be used to buy local food to serve vulnerable families. Pretty soon you have a new economy, built on local resources big enough one day to fill the gap left by king coal which is currently on life support.

As Josh Lohnes, the West Virginia University professor I spoke to in Morgantown told me, a significant public investment is required for a self-sustaining food and farm economy to emerge. "Creating a viable small farm sector is difficult because of all the challenges required to secure land, working capital, and the necessary skills," he told me. "To reach our potential we need a hefty, five-year support program for new farmers." He also made it clear that food banks were not receiving enough money or donated food to meet the demand, and that they needed more support as well. And to stress the potential of connecting food assistance to the local food economy, he cited the example of the Community Food Innovation Center in Morgantown, which includes a business that prepares meals for daycare centers and the Child and Adult Care Food program that receives federal meal reimbursements.

But a new economy also requires new people, especially ones that are young, entrepreneurial, and energetic. As Erik Johnson from the Huntington-based Facing Hunger Food Bank told me, there is a lack of incentives for young people to stay and come to West Virginia, especially to the core of what is known as Appalachia. "You have an oligarchy, politically and otherwise, that's almost like a caste system that rules things here. When it comes to getting things done, it's very much of a 'who you know' culture." About the same age as Gabe, and similarly earnest about the need for social and economic change, Erik sees a "young, liberal contingent emerging [in WV] who could take on the elite," as he likes to describe them.

One place where youth of all ages have seized control in West Virginia is its world-renowned music and dance festival scene. In addition to its natural beauty, the state excels like nowhere else when it comes to drawing pickers and stompers from across the globe. As a kind of Motown of the Mountains, numerous music and dance genres from fiddle to banjo, blue grass to traditional, clogging to square dance, storytelling to mournful ballads that ooze their own brand of Scotch–Irish soul have washed over the state for 200 years leaving unique tracks from hollows to ridgelines. The contemporary outlet for all of this comes to a head during the warm months when festivals sprout like ramps in the state's humid forests and fields. Tents and do-it-yourself parking lots turn previously peaceful villages and grassy slopes into secular revival meetings where the worship of 24/7 revelry is the only sacrament. Bearded men and braided lasses—

young, old, and in between—create a Bruegelian canvas where limber bodies prance, and instruments, sometimes "melted and warped" by the omnipresent dampness, wail day and night. Weed and whiskey are by no means discouraged, but unlike the last music festival I attended fifty-four years ago—the vague memory of which certifies that I was present—the West Virginia stimulants are placed in service to a more active and participatory role for all concerned.

I know all this only because my thirty-something son, Peter, has attended many West Virginia festivals. The Appalachian String Band Music Festival is one such event that takes place in early August in the tiny Fayette County town of Clifftop which, apropos of its name, sits high above the New River Gorge. "Clifftop," the place that also serves as the festival's unofficial name, draws over 3,000 people for five days of camping, music, dance, and an all-round celebration of America's purist folk traditions. For a grand sum of fifty bucks, you can camp as long as you want and gain access to all the goings-on which toggle back and forth between scheduled stage acts to a spontaneous eruption of fiddle music at four in the morning. "There's basically a small window between five and seven a.m.," Peter tells me, "When the site is pretty much quiet, but otherwise there's always music and movement." And just to remind my Woodstock generation what we can longer do, he says, "After hanging out with friends, playing and listening to music all day, dancing until five in the morning, and feeling a bit hungover, we might hike the steep two-mile trail down to the New River to swim and bath. Then we hike back up." At least he's not getting there by jumping off the bridge.

Back at New Roots, I'm sipping a beer and enjoying the evening light falling across the various green shades and rows of vegetable plants. The farm's story of transition from the privately owned Whitlock Farm that ceased operation in 2005 to today's non-profit community enterprise—the land title being held now by the national Agrarian Trust in cooperation with the Agrarian Commons—is one that demonstrates unusual public foresight. West Virginia counties have the option of establishing farmland boards and assessing a small property transaction fee to fund the purchase of farmland in fee or as a conservation easement. It was through such a fund that Fayette County bought the Whitlock property (Gabe and the Farm's production manager, Susan Wheeler, were both working for the county at the time the deal was done) and, while other uses for the site such as a school were considered, it was determined in 2016 that the land should be preserved and used as a farm. With the formation of the non-profit New Roots Community Farm, the land was dedicated to agricultural use, community service, and education.

Perhaps, because of the generous impulse of the county and community it serves, the public benefit to which the land was directed, or the way a lovingly tended farm settles even the most rambunctious of hearts, that one New Roots farmer said, "this is the coolest place I've ever been!" Similar sentiments were echoed as we broke bread and gnawed chicken wings together in the farm's barn on a warm summer night. Almost all of the young staff are from out of state; they initially came to test their mettle against category 5 whitewater rapids and formidable rock faces, and most of them are women.

But because people can't live by adventure alone, they showed a more tender and other-directed side as well when speaking of why they were drawn to the farm as a place to work. One young man shared his story of being a para-medic during the height of COVID-19 and losing part of his hearing due to the extreme physical conditions he was forced to work under. For him, New Roots was first a place of refuge, followed by healing, and now a place that is setting a stage for a career in farming. A woman said she "thinks a lot about community and class—who gets to eat what and why; that's what gets me fired up. Feed the people! Food is a human right!" Another young woman said, "The smallest crack in the door that exposes you to farming is one of the great joys of being alive. I want to be that crack in the door for those who haven't experienced the wonder and joys and the bodily euphoria of having that experience."

A modest note of defiance also reverberated around the table, as if there was a felt need to justify their choice of farming as a serious occupation. "I may not care if society doesn't regard what we do [here] as viable within a capitalistic framework," said one woman, adding ironically, "I'm so glad I don't have a real job!" Another woman echoed that statement with a rhetorical question, "What's the standard of success in this country? Make money. Work for the right company. In other words, society's definition of rewards is not consistent with farming's." A young man added, "Farming is connected to my quality of life. Food self-reliance, small trading groups, and a sense of community are my standards of success."

By the force of its mission, accompanied by its inspiring surroundings, New Roots has managed to attract an impressive vanguard of new farmers committed to building a sustainable future on the ground of a withering past. They are clear-eyed young people who are braced by strong values that uphold their own independence. Yet, at the same time, they embrace a sense of solidarity with each other that is collectively motivated by a shared goal to serve a community. Comfortable with the irony of serving themselves at the same time they serve others, they find a special kinship with New Roots, itself a hybrid non-profit, for-profit model of how you organize yourself in a world that's not tolerant of too much deviation. It is informed by a belief that you must take care of yourself, pay attention to your passions, don't accept the status quo when it ceases to be useful, but hold on to that moral compass, which will guide you to a higher good.

Bringing younger generations to Fayette and Mingo Counties, as well as the entire state of West Virginia, is required for the state to survive and eventually thrive. The kind of innovation that I saw from young-ish leaders like Gabe Pena and Facing Hunger's Erik Johnson and Cyndi Kirkhart, supported by engaged and visionary academics like Joshua Lohnes, are the essential play makers for change. But their efforts won't be worth a bushel of ramps without a robust, forward-looking public sector investment. "Feed the people!" is more than a fist-raised-high slogan, it's sound economic policy that serves multiple bottom lines: it promotes food security and healthy diets, puts land into production for the people who make up the states hundreds of mostly rural communities, attracts smart, hard-working young people like those at New Roots, and diversifies an economy that has relied on extractive industries that were never more than a bad deal with the devil.

Besides the models and energy that I was witness to, there are other building blocks already in place. West Virginia's festival scene raises up local economies as well as a cultural heritage that is second to none. Tourism captures the imagination of active outdoors people as well as those who want to quietly enjoy that state's beauty. Interestingly, existing federal food assistance commitments can be creatively deployed to feed, nourish, and plant a new food economy rather than simply flood the coffers of Walmart and Kroger. As one young New Roots farmer told us, "I want to connect over food." West Virginia's food system offers connections galore!

CHAPTER THREE

Laredo Shows the Way to a Mending Wall

July, 2023

In America's most Hispanic city, sitting hard against the Mexican border, you'll find imaginative city leaders, entrepreneurial non-profits, community-minded for-profits, and a vital international, cross-border economy that benefits everyone except the people who live there. In spite of the massive volumes of produce that cross from Mexico into Texas each day, the city's people encounter food insecurity, food deserts, and a host of diet-related health problems at levels far above average. But youth, partnerships, and an abundance of creativity show promise of lifting this community to new heights. Biggest surprise: Binational River Park.

... Before I built a wall I'd ask to know
What I was walling in or walling out
And to whom I was like to give offense.
Something there is that doesn't love a wall,
That wants it down.
"Mending Wall" by Robert Frost

Laredo, Texas is one of the more unique cities I have visited. Despite the fact that the Urban Dictionary defines the name as "a place you should leave," or the weird YouTube video of a faux country cowboy singer sucking as much sentimentality out of its three syllables as he can, Laredo is a fast growing, Rio Grande-flowing, border-boogeying kind of place.

Celebrating the two-hundred-and-sixty-eighth year of its founding, Laredo is drenched in a rich Spanish/Mexican/US history about which most Americans are clueless. That ignorance, when combined with its border location directly across the river from its Mexican sister city, Nuevo Laredo, sometimes turns this part of the world into a cauldron, to which the witches of the right add ingredients like eye of Newt, toe of Trump, and gall of Green. This venomous stew is then served up to the American public to heighten their fears. With their toil and trouble sown, the likes of Rep. Lauren Boebert, co-pilot with Rep. Margorie Taylor Greene of the Spaceship Looney-Tune, pronounced "President Biden's negligence of duty has resulted in the surrender of operational control of the border to the complete and total control of foreign criminal cartels putting the lives of American citizens in jeopardy." Worrisome stuff indeed, especially if any of it was true.

Without considering the source of this mischief, I too became anxious. Going to Laredo this past May for the second time in five years to work with the Laredo Food Policy Council, I wasn't sure whether to have my bullet-proof vest dry-cleaned to take with me. With the expiration of the Trump perversion of Title 42, the news media projected that hordes of desperate immigrants would be flooding the "poorly protected" border. To the contrary, I arrived in Laredo to a scene of utter tranquility where even the Border Patrol looked bored. The only thing I was assaulted by was my Verizon international calling plan that hit me with an extra $10 a day charge, falsely insisting that I was in Mexico even though my hotel was a good 100 yards inside Texas.

When I asked Laredo City Councilwoman Melissa Cigarroa, a staunch anti-wall advocate, why there wasn't more visible commotion, she immediately called the Republican assertions of chaos at the border "nonsense," then offered that it was part of a Trump-inspired narrative that "Laredo is a dangerous place filled with dirty migrants crossing at will." Viviana Frank-Franco, born in

Mexico and a co-founder of both the Laredo Food Policy Council and the architecture firm Able City, was equally astonished when I asked her if the two-day Food Policy Council conference might be canceled. She promptly replied that "nothing is wrong; everything is quiet; it's all a bunch of hype."

The Border, NAFTA, and Many Trucks

Once a sleepy Texas town with a population in the tens of thousands, Laredo has exploded to about 270,000 today due to what is now the largest inland port in America annually channeling $227 billion in trade between Mexico and the US. Expected to climb well past 300,000 people over the next ten years, Laredo is coming to terms with the upside and downside of its growth as well as the all-pervasive border security industrial complex. Its binational status and vibrant cultural heritage offer endless life-enhancing possibilities, while its extreme climate issues like deep drought and withering heat (it's 108 °F in Laredo as I'm writing this in late June) may alter life for the worse.

In order to make Laredo an inland port—a product of the North American Free Trade Agreement (NAFTA)—a multi-lane highway and bridge were constructed connecting Nuevo Laredo, Mexico to Laredo, Texas. Now known as Interstate 35, this transportation network, along with rail lines, conveys thousands of trucks a day right through the heart of the city.

Free trade, as they say, is only "free" for the private companies that benefit from government subsidies, but very costly for those who are smack-dab in the path of its development. The massive infrastructure required to build the port blew away the homes of 390 Laredo residents who had the poor fortune of living in the way of "progress." The belching diesels and other trade traffic leave a King Kong-size carbon footprint; much of the cargo passing in sight of Laredo neighborhoods is fresh produce from Mexican fields, none of which is available to the people who live there; and the border security with its lights, gates, and armed keepers suggest Checkpoint Charlie in the Cold War-divided city of Berlin where the US faced off against the Soviet Union, not the friendly nation of Mexico. This present-day reality stands in stark contrast to what

Frank recalls when she would cross the border frequently fifty years ago as a child: "We'd refer to it as 'going to the other side.' There was one border guard on the bridge who you smiled at and waved to."

The Emerging Food System

In contrast to this rough and tumble economic growth, Laredo is progressively and thoughtfully nurturing a robust and more just food system, much-needed in light of the city's high poverty rate (25 percent) and distressing diet-related health numbers. Set against its bustling inland port, Laredo is not only joining the urban trend of cool new coffee shops and boutique Japanese restaurants, it's also raising up locally produced food as evidenced by a farmers' market and young new farmers like Marcella Juarez; encouraging the development of micro-food businesses like @houseofbreadd which makes gluten-free/sugar-free baked goods; addressing the gaps in healthy, affordable food retail with the emerging Frontera Grocery Coop; and harnessing public policy for healthy change under the city's dynamic, young new health department head, Dr. Richard Chamberlain.

During a panel discussion on the second day of the Food Policy Council conference, Dr. Chamberlain, nattily attired in a sharp blue suit, highlighted by a pair of bright white fashion sneaks, shared the sobering findings of his department's city-wide health assessment (Texas Health Institute, n.d.). "Thirty-two percent of the respondents reported that they were unable to eat nutritious food due to lack of money," he noted with concern. But even more worrisome was the diet-related health data. Laredo's obesity rate was over 45 percent with an official diabetes prevalence of 15.7 percent, figures that are far in excess of both Texas and US averages. Putting a challenge to the 100 or so people gathered at the event, Dr. Chamberlain said, "These numbers are a call to action! We need a collective voice to drive policy decisions."

Later, I spoke with Councilwoman Cigarroa, who, as a local policy maker, is in a position to address these unfortunate numbers. "I don't know a family that's not impacted by diabetes, which is a particularly pernicious disease," she said, adding that her husband has been practicing cardiology in Laredo for decades and sees lots of heart disease stemming from diet. Of Mexican-American heritage herself, Cigarroa doesn't hesitate to blame part of the problem on "traditional Mexican food choices that are [from a health perspective] mostly terrible." But she also makes it clear that Laredo is medically underserved, and, as the assessment points out, about 30 percent of the residents are uninsured. A large number of undocumented people are also reluctant to seek medical care when they're sick. "I know too many men who stay at home rather than get help when they have a shooting pain in their shoulder," she says, "They say it's nothing to worry about; it's just indigestion."

Cigarroa makes it clear that at least another leg of Laredo's health stool is physical activity. For instance, the heat can be so punishing in the warm weather months that nobody wants to go outside to exert themselves. In driving around Laredo for two days, I also noticed a severe absence of parks. She confirmed my observations, pointing out that the health assessment process heard that problem loud and clear from residents. The study's methodology included numerous surveys that ranked the community's concerns, including the finding that, "Over a quarter (26 percent) of community survey respondents indicated that a lack of parks and playgrounds is a problem affecting their health or the health of those with whom they live."

Binational River Park

A good part of the answer to the lack of safe, multi-use public space may come from the very place that generates much of the region's tension—the border. At the beginning of 2022, the US and Mexico jointly announced that they intend to create the Binational River Conservation Park that will be a 6.3-mile corridor along the Rio Grande (US name)/Rio Bravo (Mexican name). As a non-walled or fenced 1,000-acre park that incorporates the river, it will join Laredo and Nuevo Laredo. Multiple agencies and government levels are responsible for making this visionary project happen, but US Ambassador to Mexico, Kenneth Salazar (former US Interior Secretary), is receiving much of the applause (Binational River Park, n.d.).

As a project with a $100 million price tag, not only is the Binational River Conservation Park cheaper than Trump's vanity wall priced at $24 million per mile, it will incorporate over forty projects such as a monarch butterfly garden since the park is along the monarch's flyway, a tree farm, a job training site for various outdoor trades, and numerous cultural, educational, and recreational activities. The project "walls" nothing out; it offers a bridge of peace and humanity to all, and in the words of Frank Rotnofsky, co-founder of Able City architects and one of the project's primary design firms, "This is a once-in-a-lifetime project for planners and architects!"

From Councilwoman Cigarroa's perspective, the Park builds beautifully on Laredo's number one natural asset, the Rio Grande. But as one who can barely contain her disdain for Trump and his wall—Cigarroa was the board president of the No Border Wall coalition for several years—she sees any security wall as both an environmental and security failure—it destroys natural wildlife corridors, but also, ironically, fails to keep people out. "Not only does Laredo currently not have a wall, it has the lowest illegal crossing rate anywhere along the border, including places like El Paso that do have walls," she said. As the elected official who stands as the Park's staunchest advocate, Cigarroa sees it as "an amazing opportunity" and that "it's incumbent upon the city to make it happen." She speaks to the culturally unifying theme of the park that brings the two cities—Laredo and Nuevo Laredo—together, and also to the larger purpose of creating a "highly visible, safer space in a beautiful setting that will draw people to it for productive activity." In fact, with more than a little pride in her voice, Councilwoman Cigarroa thinks the Park will one day rival the world-class San Antonio River Walk, as a destination site.

With aspirational language that embraces a new world order, the Park's website declares that:

> *The Binational River Park at the Rio Grande-Rio Bravo in Laredo and Nuevo Laredo connects and celebrates our common culture on the United States and Mexico border. It reclaims our shared history, spurs the economy, promotes security on both sides of the river, and restores the ecological treasure we call home. The first of its kind, this international conservation project enhances our quality of life and serves as a prototype for border*

cities around the world to follow. Two nations, one community. One river. One park. (Binational River Park, n.d.)

Farming

While the Park will offer a host of environmental amenities, including ones that will benefit the region's food system writ large, it doesn't eliminate the challenges that have left Laredo and its surrounding area virtually bereft of all forms of agriculture. The Food Policy Council and its partner organization, the Laredo Center for Urban Agriculture and Sustainability, are attempting to fill that yawning void with smaller-scale farms and gardens. One of the people who is opening a path to a new agricultural future for south Texas is Marcella Juarez, who, with her brother Manuel, is converting a mostly fallow 110-acre ranch known as Palo Blanco into an intensive, state-of-the heart, mixed-use food production and instructional farm. On land that has been in her family for 160 years, she hopes to make it a "foundational source of good local food for my community."

Armed with a master's degree in small scale and sustainable farming from Texas State University at San Marcos and a bright and brimming confidence that belies her twenty-something years, Marcella got the farm's new enterprises up and running at the same time COVID-19 hit. Undeterred and with a business plan that would make any banker's head spin, she started applying hydroponic science and technology, including adapted, solar-powered shipping container farms she designed herself, to the unforgiving, heat-heavy, drought-laden Laredo landscape. Her crops are a daring mix of microgreens, herbs, eggs, and sprouts for a marketplace that is, one might say, only in the tasting stage for such products. But the early reception has been enthusiastic at the farmers' market, among a few cutting-edge chefs, and with customers for their own farm-to-home delivery service. With the help of the Food Policy Council, Marcella hopes to see market demand grow steadily.

Clearly, Palo Blanco is a mission-driven enterprise. Having attended a small, rural school where her father taught, and where her friends were buying food at a gas station grocery store, Marcella decided at a young age that, "everyone deserves access to fresh food, and that I wanted to use our ranch to feed my friends." But her views extend beyond a compassion for others and a heart-felt desire to feed her community. "Hispanic people need lots of healing," she says. "As Mexicans we're just viewed as farmworkers, not farm owners. God willing, we'll have more young Hispanic farmers soon." In addition to wanting to make her community more food secure, she also recognizes its dietary health challenges. "Food is our first medicine," she said, and in a burst of authentic optimism, she added, "We're starting to see health, diet, and local food coming together!"

One new development for Texans came to light during the FPC conference that could make a difference to Laredo and young farmers like Marcella all across Texas. The Texas Department of Agriculture (TDA) had completed the "Texas Food Access Study," (Barber and Stone, 2022), which among other things recommended the establishment (passed into law in June) of a state food policy council (Texas State Food Policy Council, 2023). Count me as a skeptic when it comes to anything about Texas state government. So, when I heard about this report, I had thought for a moment that Jim Hightower had seized control of the TDA's commissioner's office under cover of darkness. While some Texas food justice advocates have rightfully criticized the study as not going far enough, in the words of Addie Stone, Policy Specialist at TDA and the study's co-author, "It's not perfect, but it's a start." I would agree with both the advocates and Stone, but, most importantly, it puts the State of Texas on record as acknowledging the state's high levels of food insecurity and their need to support locally oriented forms of agriculture and food distribution. That gives advocates and local farmers a place to build from.

A little before my ride to the airport arrived, I strolled a short distance down to the banks of the Rio Grande, a river so freighted with history and ecological significance that watching its brown waters gave me momentary shivers. It occurred to me that at least a few H_2O molecules now flowing beneath me had started their 1,896 miles journey to the Gulf of Mexico from the snow packs of the Rocky Mountains. There was a majesty of movement before me that existed far beyond my comprehension.

On the Texas bank, a few people baited hooks and lazily cast their fishing lines into the water, making audible plops in the still morning air. Across the river, not much further than I used to be able to throw a baseball, a half dozen Mexicans were also fishing, mirroring their American counterparts who, in all likelihood, were themselves of Mexican ancestry. Just upslope on the Mexican side, hanging limp in the morning calm, was the Mexican flag, so large that it could cover the entire Fenway Park infield. Upriver, a railroad bridge, a symbol of binational commerce, bisected a horizon that was largely dominated by forests and the Rio Grande's serene, narrowing perspective. It didn't escape me that this image of peace and beauty softly unwinding before me didn't allow for the unsavory actions of desperate people who may have been concealed in the bushes and bullrushes. Hurt begets hurt, and when all that you carry on your back are the twin lashes of poverty and violence, fear and flight are your closest companions.

There is an energy in Laredo coming from those associated with the Food Policy Council, city hall, and numerous private sector endeavors that holds the promise of uniting two nations, partnering on shared health and environmental concerns, and equitably distributing a steadily growing prosperity. In all likelihood, success will be determined by whether the Rio Grande is viewed as a mending force and a healing gift of nature, or as a barrier that walls people off from each other and only serves to "give offense."

CHAPTER FOUR

Roadkill Stew, Bad-ass Cabbage, and the Midnight Sun—Lessons from Alaska

July, 2016

Alaska stands out from all fifty states for its unique food system challenges and opportunities. Its long distance to what is generally known as conventional food production and distribution channels are matched only by its close proximity to an abundant, wild, and certainly unconventional sources and types of food. The injustices that have beset people of color, communities with limited resources, and the environment across the nation are revealed starkly and often uniquely throughout Alaska. In a place where self-reliance is not just an ideal but a necessity, the state has also deployed public policy and a good measure of help thy neighbor mentality to promote food security and a just form of food sovereignty. Biggest surprise: A six-feet wide cabbage.

The Alaska Airlines flight dips over Cook Inlet on its approach into Anchorage. The sunlight is reflecting off distant glaciers and the cupcake glaze of snow-topped islands. My watch tells me it's 10:30 p.m. but the midnight sun is as bright as a summer noon in New Mexico.

It's easy this time of year to be drugged by the omnipresent subpolar light and the glistening line of saw-toothed mountain peaks. Pretty soon, however, a food system guy like myself wonders how people get their food. Sure, my credit card bought me a sumptuous grilled salmon dinner, a fish so abundant in the surrounding waters that each Alaskan household is entitled to catch twenty-five big ones a year, provided you can endure standing in chest-deep, ice-cold water. So, when the thermometer hits twenty below and the food barge from Seattle is iced in; the weather is keeping bush pilots grounded and not able to service roadless villages; milk is going for $9.00 a gallon and you're salivating for some fresh greens; and yes, there's wild game everywhere but you haven't hit a live animal with a harpoon since that time you almost speared the assistant track coach with a wayward javelin toss, then what?

Alaska possesses more than its share of food system idiosyncrasies—a short growing season, beaucoup summer light, remote locations, and supply chains that stretch 4,000 miles to the lower forty-eight states. But in the course of talking with members of the Alaska Food Policy Council (Alaska Food Policy Council, n.d.) and other food system stakeholders, I began to wonder if Alaskan's unique forms of adaptation held lessons for those in gentler climes. The relationship between resiliency and climate change, links between sustainability, non-renewable energy and the social welfare system, and the role that "wild" food plays in the state's food system started to feel strangely prescient to me.

Tour de farms

Moonstone Farm

If you want a first-hand look at Alaskan agriculture, sign on to a half-day trip with Alaska Farm Tours (Alaska Farm Tours, n.d.). If you also want to experience some poignant history, sign on to their

Matanuska Valley Tour in Palmer, located about an hour northeast of Anchorage. The tour's owner/operator is the feisty—and as of this June, very pregnant—Margaret Adsit, who also works for Alaska Farmland Trust. As such, she's both knowledgeable and passionate about the state's farm scene.

You'll learn that twenty hours of daylight allows a cabbage to reach six-feet in diameter and concentrates the sugars in carrots to such a degree that it makes them insanely sweet. Think you have problems with raccoons or woodchucks? Try keeping a 1,500-pound moose from eating her way through two-acres of vegetables. And while it stands to reason that Alaskans will use season extenders like hoop houses, the state's farmers use more USDA high-tunnel subsidy funds than any other state in the country (based on personal correspondence with USDA's Alaska Farm Service Administrator).

In 1935, someone in FDR's Emergency Relief Administration got the bright idea to relocate some of the Depression's dispossessed farmers to the Matanuska Valley. Over 200 "volunteer" families from Michigan, Minnesota, and Wisconsin said goodbye to their friends and took up residence in a place where they had been promised forty acres, a house, and bulldozers to ready the glacier-carved forest land for farming. When they arrived, the land was there but nothing else. They were forced to live in tents and clear the land with horses. Within five years half of the families left their allotments, and by 1965 only twenty of the original families were still tilling the soil.

In spite of the hardships—and the unlikely prospect that the colonists would ever again vote for a Democrat—farms took root, some prospered, and today the Matanuska Valley is a little agricultural gem enveloped by a stunning ascension of snow-streaked mountains. We visited the last farm that is owned by a descendant of the original families, fifth-generation Don Church, who, with his wife Michelle, operates Moonstone Farm. On a day as exquisite as the one I saw Moonstone, transfixed by a gun-metal gray peak that appeared to breach whale-like from the far end of a sweet little hay field, for a few dangerous moments I imagined myself homesteading in such a place. But when I heard how the plastic was ripped off the greenhouse hoops by the razor-like winter wind, how human eyes can freeze shut at twenty below, and that the catcher's mitt-sized hoofs of a moose can turn rows of carefully nurtured vegetables into zucchini pulp, I quickly let go of the fantasy.

The Role of Subsistence

There are only 750 farms in Alaska. Even with the addition of a small portion of Alaska's $4 billion commercial seafood catch (the vast majority is exported), Alaska must import over 90 percent of its food. In its premiere issue released this June *Edible Alaska* (Edible Alaska, n.d.) spotlights a farmer who uses float planes to transport goats, and another who must wait for high tide before he can motor his skiff filled to the gunwales with produce to market. Though gyrations like these don't compensate for Alaska's shortage of agricultural advantages, its ecosystem makes up for it by setting nature's feast before those who can hunt, fish, and gather. "Wild food," as it is called, is at the core of what Alaskans recognize as subsistence, which is defined by the Alaska Department of Fish and Game (Alaska Department of Fish and Game, n.d.) as the "customary and traditional uses of wild resources for food, clothing, [and] fuel ... "

Marylynne Kostick, a soft-spoken research analyst with the Subsistence Division, gave me a tutorial on this complicated and contentious subject. Though blessed with the physique of a runway model, Marylynne's skill sets suggest she's more at home in the woods than in the fashion world. When she's not preparing charts that explain the hunting breakdown between land and sea mammals, she devotes her free time to sun drying fish, rendering bear fat, and stretching moose hides. She shows me a photo of a beautiful bowl of food she calls "roadkill hare stew" which she explains is "another aspect of the 'food system' that shouldn't be discounted. With so many wild vehicle drivers ... and the hare population on an up cycle this year, the poor things are under attack .... Best to take them home and teach some kids to properly care for and inspect a wild animal." (I later discovered that about 800 Alaskan moose die annually from collisions with motor vehicles. Various organizations (Alaska Moose Federation, n.d.) in Alaska have stepped up to remove, process, and distribute the meat from these poor critters to charitable feeding sites.)

Through numbers and words, Marylynne makes it clear that "wild foods" are a critical part of rural Alaska's diet. Taken together, she tells me that walrus, seal, whale, sea lions, moose, caribou, bears, Dall sheep, mountain goats, and of course fish and shellfish, provide rural Alaskans (125,000 people or 17 percent of the state's population) with an average of 189 percent of their protein and 26 percent of their caloric intake. The absence of any reliable pricing makes it difficult to determine the market value of this food, but using estimates of between $4 and $8 per pound, the range in 2012 was between $147 million and $295 million per year.

The conflicts surrounding wild foods stem from their dietary importance and a competition from non-subsistence uses such as sports hunting and commercial fishing. As Marylynne explained to me, a big part of her division's job is to make recommendations to the state's regulatory boards that will determine who can harvest what animal using which method, and where and when they can do it. Making the task even more difficult are federal subsistence regulations that further complicate the game of wildlife management. And, in Alaska, subsistence users who are primarily Native Alaskan and rural have the highest claim, and as such "their rights would trump those of sports and commercial users," in the event that the fish and game population dropped below subsistence levels. So far, this hasn't happened.

But like the swelling chords of a cello that signal the approach of some dark force, Alaskans are starting to hear ominous notes of climate change floating ashore. While still somewhat anecdotal, those who gather wild berries, another favorite "wild food," are reporting that the harvest of some varieties has moved twenty-five miles north due to warming temperatures. A species or two of fish common to more southerly waters are starting to appear off Alaska's coast. And those who hunt walrus say it's getting harder to do so due to the absence of ice floes on which the sea mammal perches.

In one curious twist on indigenous peoples' cultural practices, food banks are becoming popular above the Arctic Circle, a region where the wild food harvest equals 438 pounds per person. Why? Native hunters have a spiritual connection to their prey. If the animal doesn't "present itself" to the hunter, as if to say "I am allowing you to take me to feed your family" then the gun is not fired nor is the harpoon released. According to some people I spoke with, Native Alaskans may be turning away from subsistence hunting in favor of the food bank because it is "presenting itself" to the people in the same way that a hunted animal would.

Concerns arise as well around the future of Alaska's limited farmland. Development pressure is keen and during the tour of the popular Matanuska Valley it became obvious where future housing would go—on farmland which is fetching $20,000 to $30,000 per acre.

Another potential fall from grace has been playing itself out in the state's legislature this year. Since 1973 Alaskan residents have benefited from the creation of the Alaska Permanent Fund Dividend (PFD) (State of Alaska, Department of Revenue, n.d.) which was the state's way of sharing the North Slope's oil wealth. Not only were state government's coffers filled by the revenues, each Alaskan received an annual check averaging around $2,000. This wealth distribution scheme has been credited by some economists with giving Alaska a more equal wage distribution (less income inequality) than the rest of the US. However, state revenues have fallen precipitously in response to falling oil prices, plunging the state into a budget crisis, one that is likely to drastically reduce the PFD. The lesson, I suppose, is that what oil giveth, oil taketh away, to say nothing of what oil leaveth behind in the form of more carbon emissions.

Still, like everywhere else, the local food movement shines across Alaska bright as the midnight sun. Communities in this vast state are creatively maximizing their man-made and mother nature-made resources. The Alaska Food Policy Council has had success with legislative and administrative action to support the growth of the local food economy. There's even been progress in social justice, not a field in which Alaska typically excels. According to Sarra Khlifi of the Alaska Food Coalition (Alaska Food Coalition, n.d.), a group affiliated with both the Food Policy Council and the Food Bank of Alaska, the legislature this year suspended a lifetime ban on food stamp eligibility for convicted drug felons, surely a draconian measure if there ever was one.

How Alaska copes with its multiple food system vulnerabilities bears watching. Resiliency in the face of climate change will take on new and challenging dimensions in this highly exposed northern reach, not the least of which may be the hot, sweaty hordes escaping from the Lower 48. The lessons of oil, the lessons of subsistence, the lessons of the limits of human endurance, and the lessons of public policy that can be farsighted or shortsighted should not be ignored because they come from a place as remote as Alaska.

CHAPTER FIVE

Huerta del Valle—An Ontario Oasis

August, 2015

The power of food to build community and change lives, especially in the midst of rampant environmental injustice, is revealed at this urban agriculture site in a Latino neighborhood in southern California. But beyond the yearning of people to gain a measure of control over their circumstances, we find inspired local leadership and an alliance with eager and often well-resourced partners capable of helping a worthwhile start-up get through those inevitable rough patches. Biggest surprise: I like Zumba!

What is the sound of women's hands slapping tortillas into shape? Is it water falling over a rocky stream bed? Or a series of slaps across your face? Maybe it's a doctor's swop across a new-born baby's bum reminding it that life has begun? Whatever it resembles, the sound of the human hand on food, combined with the arousing scent of sizzling, freshly herbed vegetables, announce that a small feast is about to begin beneath the pop-up canopies where we sit.

The summer sun is sinking just behind the compost pile massed at the western edge of Huerta del Valle (Huerta del Valle, n.d.), a community garden located in the flight path of the Ontario, California, airport. It is three-and-a-half acres packed with lush green plants and rainbow shades of produce, and it's a place that ripples with a near-divine sense of community where the Spanish chatter of women is so richly woven into the air around us that it somehow softens the scream of the Southwest 737 accelerating overhead.

Maria Alonso presides over Huerta del Valle with the countenance of a gentle priest—available, affable, affectionate; never insistent nor hovering. Though the daughter of a Mexican farming family, she tells me that she always managed to find a hiding place whenever her father summoned her to the field. But like millions of parents of the past decades, it took a child with a health condition that might be remedied through a new diet to bring her enthusiastically back to the soil. In Maria's case it was her ADHD son, and a doctor with the imagination to "prescribe" unprocessed, chemical-free food that changed Maria's life. Lacking land and the means to buy retail organic food, she set about the task of organizing a community garden so she could "grow her own" and help others do the same.

The first site was on a piece of Ontario public school land that could only accommodate fifteen gardeners. But Maria's community of healthy food eaters was growing rapidly and needed something larger. Working with a very cooperative city planning department and the Healthy Ontario Collaborative, not only did Huerta find their current site, they found funding support from Kaiser Permanente and institutional support from nearby Pitzer College which, coincidentally, was also offering their students food justice courses. Huerta was a practicum made in heaven!

The Pitzer connection would eventually bring money, produce sales, and eager volunteers to the bourgeoning Huerta project, but most importantly it brought a recent graduate, Arthur Levine. Arthur is Maria's sidekick, confidant, and, as a fluent Spanish-speaker, sometimes he's her translator. Brooklyn-born and bred, Arthur doesn't have an agrarian background, but tells me, "My mother is a chef and a stay-at-home mom who taught me to love and value those who work in food, grow the food, cook the food and provide for the most necessary needs of life." You could say this love found further expression in his growing passion for social and economic justice which "are amazing and worth fighting for," not by smashing Wal-Mart, he assures me, but by "building the world we want to see, and that really works for everyone." One might reasonably argue that Arthur's path to Huerta was preordained.

Nestled into a densely packed, mostly Latino neighborhood of small, tidy homes, Huerta del Valle shares a border with a pleasant town park that is also home to a vibrant community center. However, I'm forced to lean closer to Maria so I can hear her over the roar of a descending jet airliner. Giant commercial warehouses and the airport's service industries dominate the neighborhood's fringe. These structures are fed and disgorged by a constant convoy of trucks spewing diesel fumes on their way to and from nearby I-10. When the wind blows just right, petro-chemical odors from two plastic molding factories overwhelm the scent of the garden's cilantro. Warehouse jobs—a source of many occupational injuries—and the construction industry's ruthless quest to conquer California's landscape with McMansions are the community's primary employers. I guess this is what passes for affordable housing policy in America—we keep housing prices low with the help of environmental injustice.

It's no surprise then that Maria's community of friends, family, and neighborhood residents seek refuge at Huerta del Valle. They are not refugees fleeing an imminent threat so much as pilgrims seeking the joy of each other's company and the earthly delights of a beautiful place. At present, sixty-two families tend garden plots (there are fifteen families on a waiting list; it's estimated that each family plot generates $15 a week in food savings). Two, half-acre plots are managed independently by three urban farmers—Andres, Eugenio, and Gonzalo—as part of Huerta's effort to explore the commercial potential of urban farming. These small farming businesses are assisted by garden staff who market their harvest at three community farmers' markets, one CSA, seven area restaurants and the Pitzer dining hall. That, plus several hundred volunteers, dozens of school groups, and assorted WWOOFers from as far away as China, Colombia, Austria, Germany, and Sweden make up what is a robust and multi-functional use of this peri-urban land.

Huerta's numbers are as impressive as the bounty of its plots. Having seen more than my fair share of community gardening enterprises I would have to place this one at the very top of my qualitative and aesthetic ranking. But, as I've said before, the most important word in community gardening is not gardening. And it is in the world of community building where Huerta definitely excels.

"This is my community," Maria says to me in a loving, non-possessive way. "I hear from the gardeners all the time how the 'garden makes us feel better,' and that 'I don't feel depressed in the garden,' and that 'the garden is my family and my therapy.'" She goes on to relate one heart-wrenching tale of a woman who was leaving her abusive and heavy-drinking husband after twenty-three years, and who told her, "'I need change in my life, Maria. You can give me the power to change.'" Community organizer, gardening coach, and Mother Confessor are the skills Maria employs that nourish the garden far better than any fertilizer could.

As Huerta's principal salesman, Arthur describes for me their unconventional marketing strategy, which consists of one part community engagement and what economists might informally call the Robin Hood wealth redistribution model. On Saturday morning the surrounding community can buy produce at the garden itself for $1 per pound; Pitzer College might buy the same produce at $2.50 per pound; and high-end restaurants may buy it for $4 per pound. I understood as well that there were one or two "elite buyers" who were *permitted* to pay $8 per pound.

While this "pricing policy" might not fit the ideal of market-place transparency, everyone participating in this Ontario-based value chain seems happy with its values. From the family gardeners who donate their surplus to the "common marketing pool" to those at the top of the region's food chain—including some very talented and progressive chefs—Huerta is creatively and collectively starting to generate a modest revenue stream.

But just because Maria and Arthur have strong community building and entrepreneurial instincts doesn't mean they don't also have to hunt for grant funding. The project's start-up funds are diminishing, which have reduced Maria's monthly stipend to only $1,100 for what amounts to a full-time job. Though the City of Ontario and Pitzer have been generous contributors—both in-kind and cash—Huerta del Valle recently submitted a grant application to USDA's Community Food Projects grant program, which, if successful,* would allow Huerta to fully set its sails. This might enable Maria to begin work on her vision of a "community garden every mile," a beguiling concept that would site community gardens at one-mile intervals in a hub and spoke pattern radiating out from Huerta del Valle.

Feeling a bit over-fed by the loving attention of women who thought I wasn't eating enough, I accepted Arthur's invitation for a guided garden tour. I'm escorted along 100-feet rows of purple basil and habaneros; kale whose productive life has extended across a southern California growing season from October of 2014 through this July; and long borders of stone-fruit trees, sunflowers, and melons. Competing herbal scents are everywhere; my eyes lavish attention on the ascending rows of horticultural perfection and the subtle shifting of green hues. But suddenly my Anglo ears are assaulted by a powerful blast of pulsating Latin music. Noting my startled look, Arthur assures me that everything is all right: "It's six o'clock. That's when Huerta's Zumba class begins."

Somewhere near the tomatoes, on an improvised workout platform of assembled wooden pallets, the hips, arms, and shoulders of a dozen women of all shapes and sizes are gyrating to an insistent, sensual beat. They are trying, with varying degrees of success, to follow the lead of their instructor, who's urging her pupils on to ever greater feats of Zumbic glory. I'm mesmerized by the motion and music, tempted to join in but ultimately restrained by my WASPish self-consciousness. Yet I'm suspended in the moment of what, by all accounts, is the essence of community, a place where love, health, physical activity, and an aching need to connect find union. Wouldn't one of these spaced apart every mile be the answer to most of life's complications? While I contemplate an answer, I feel my hips start to sway; my taste buds relive the delights of a homemade, home-grown meal, and the California twilight fades to night.

---

*The following year Huerta del Valle won a multi-year Community Food Projects Competitive Grant Program grant.

CHAPTER SIX

Where's the Rage?

July, 2011

When you think of Seattle, you think of glittering tech-induced prosperity and a robust, diverse food scene. But with the ups and downs in the economy and the perennial lack of affordable housing, an ever-increasing number of people are driven into the arms of community food banks. The one featured here stands out for its comprehensive delivery of services as well as for the strength that it both takes and gives to its community. Yet, as the food bank gets bigger and better, the problems and demands for help only grow, and the question remains: Is charity, no matter how well-rendered, justice? And what is the role of the wealthy and public policy in not just reducing hunger, but in finally achieving justice? Biggest surprise: The everlasting capacity of people to find a reason to believe.

Dan and Isabelle sit patiently on the folding metal chairs in the tastefully decorated waiting room of Seattle's Ballard Food Bank. Intelligent, soft-spoken, and in his late fifties, Dan is a chronically underemployed architectural draftsman who barely managed to eke out three days of temporary work over the past week.

His unemployment benefits have long since evaporated and he's thinking about applying for food stamps, although he cringes as the words leave his mouth. With his shrunken income dedicated to keeping a roof over his head, he and Isabelle are two among 1,200 or so neighborhood residents who will request a shopping cart full of food this week at the food bank.

Peggy Bailey, Ballard's Operation Manager, is one of those dedicated, unflappable souls whose work holds the lives of others together as their larger universe spins out of control. Her recitation of statistics is the "growth" story that you'll hear from any of the 60,000 emergency food sites across America. "In 2001 we were serving about 350 people per week; four years ago, it was 450; now we're serving between 1,100 and 1,200." Peggy escorts me past tattooed skateboarders, young women clutching babies, and unshaven men for whom a good night is a dry patch of grass underneath a bridge.

Like all the twenty-five volunteers (out of a total of 100) on hand this day—good neighbors who keep the flow of people safe and dignified—Peggy beams with pride over the food, large walk-in refrigerators, and the recently retrofitted 6,200-square-foot former machine shop that's been their new home for only a year (after relocating from their cramped, dilapidated home of nearly forty years). Almost half of the available food is produce, some of which comes from nearby Pea Patch community gardens and local fruit tree gleaners. An abundant supply of artisan bread, fresh dairy products, and even enough frozen meat to give each person two packages, fill the shelves. Not only can you select from a rather remarkable range of products, e.g., microwaveable entrées that retail for $9.00 at Trader Joes, there's also a "no-cook" section that, in an average month, serves 350 people without kitchens. In addition, nearly 100 bags are assembled and delivered weekly to shut-ins and people with special dietary needs.

Unlike food banks in days of yore, Ballard does more than give away food. If you don't have a permanent address, they'll act as your personal post office box, a service currently used by 480 people. Case workers from the Department of Social and Health Services try to connect food bank users with SNAP (food stamps) as well as medical and dental services. Need help paying your rent or electrical bill? You can apply for a $300 voucher for the former and $200 voucher for the latter.

When I asked Peggy how she keeps up with the demand for food, she told me, almost blithely, that enough food was not a problem. In a comment that would make her the envy of every food bank worker in America, she said, "We've never had to turn anyone away due to lack of food. This is a very generous community. We have Whole Foods, Trader Joes, Safeway and dozens of other food donors." While supporting five paid staff, three trucks, and a good-size modern facility, the food bank gets 95 percent of its operating funds from private donations, receiving only $40,000 per year from Seattle city government. One anonymous individual, for instance, gives the Ballard Food Bank $2,000 each month just to buy fresh dairy products.

In contrast to the generosity of the surrounding neighborhoods, you have the US House of Representatives. If the miracles that these Seattle residents pull off every day remind you of Christ's feeding of the 5,000, the House majority's proposal to slash $3 billion from SNAP, WIC, and TEFAP is decidedly Scrooge-like. At a time when the nation's economy is still on life support and when a record 43 million Americans are receiving food stamps, the House Republicans want to hack the safety net with a machete while leaving the silver cutlery of hedge fund operators untarnished. Take from the poor, but don't touch a dime of the rich.

Ballard is a human-scale urban environment whose sloping topography gently lowers you to the shores of the Puget Sound. On street corners, food bank volunteers greet the homeless people by name, who, in turn, respond in a friendly manner, pleased that there are people who don't avert their eyes. Stroll a few blocks north of Market Street, and you'll come to a lovely park where grassy slopes and park benches are populated by homeless men catching a ray or two of Seattle's stingy sunlight. In the opposite corner is a small skateboard tunnel where young dudes, hat brims cocked at precise angles, practice their chutes and curls. Between the skaters and the homeless are several fountains that spray giggling toddlers cheered on by happy moms.

The park reflects Ballard's values: there's room for everybody, diversity is encouraged, and the community does its darnedest to meet everyone's needs. But, beneath this cloak of tolerance, there is a creeping sense that there may be limits to what any group of caring people can do. Perhaps it's symbolized by the police cruiser stationed just across the street from the "homeless end" of the park. Maybe you hear it in the voices of the young men at the food pantry who were too ashamed to give me their names, but did say that in spite of a couple of years of college they couldn't find jobs. "We're not trained for anything." Or perhaps you can smell it on the breath of the middle-aged drunken man, who according to Peggy had been "doing so well up until now."

If the House Republicans have their way, the Ballard Food Bank's waiting room could very well become so crowded that the smiling volunteers will be replaced by stern-faced security guards. When I asked John, an eighty-seven-year-old food bank volunteer of twelve years, what he thought was behind the ever-rising number of clients, he said emphatically, "It's all about the economy. I see how embarrassed people are who are asking for help, but you can either sleep on the street or come to the food bank." One has to ask if that is the vision that the budget cutting, non-taxing conservative minority have for America. If that is true, and every statement from the Republican leadership seems to suggest that it is, then one has to ask where the rage is at this time in our nation's history.

How big must food banks get to contain the ever-swelling legions of un- and underemployed workers? How much food will Ballard's neighborhood grocers have to donate to ensure that all the young mothers can feed themselves as well as their babies? Is there indeed a tipping point when community compassion can no longer clean up the mess made by mean-spirited politicians who avert their eyes from the growing victims of a failed American Dream?

Evelyn, eighty-seven, has been volunteering at the Ballard Food Bank for fifteen years, longer than anyone else. She's a feisty, retired machinist who worked for a Boeing Aircraft subcontractor. Sitting at a table where she was sorting nuts into small plastic bags for the home delivery sacks, Evelyn shared the most commonly expressed reason for volunteering at food banks. "If you've been blessed, you have to give back." Yes, I said, I'd heard that sentiment from many people in the emergency food world, but I wondered if there wasn't something else. At that point the fiery machinist union member took over from the charitable grandmother. Growing up during the Great Depression on a Minnesota farm, she did not need the reason for rage explained to her. "Things have to change in this country," she said, eyes narrowing and pronouncing each syllable more distinctly. "The idea of not taxing the rich is ridiculous. We have to stop farm and oil subsidies. We got to get politicians to care about people all the time, not just when they're trying to get elected."

Compassion and "giving back" may not be sustainable when one class of Americans lives under the House Republicans' Golden Fleece, while bourgeoning flocks find shelter under highway overpasses. So that compassion may live, we must sometimes release the rage.

CHAPTER SEVEN

Troubled by Paradise

August, 2011

Like Alaska, Hawai'i has its own unique challenges to food sovereignty and self-reliance. Much of these are due to the dispossession of land, overdevelopment, and erasure of traditional cultural practices including diet. In the face of these injustices, advocates and funders could have only pursued food-related solutions, but instead they demonstrated the leadership and imagination that plumbed deeper roots. Building a new generation of well-trained and motivated young leaders through farming—not for farming—was their goal. Biggest surprise: Mai Tais are stronger than I thought, and Hawai'i's poverty is deeper than I realized.

The rum-soaked beverage and balmy breeze were starting to erode my leftist resistance to luxury. Let's face it, sipping a Mai Tai from a beachfront terrace with a billion-dollar view of Diamond Head will dull the edge of the most hardened class warrior. But just as I was slouching into vacation mode, I made the mistake of cracking open Sarah Vowell's *Unfamiliar Fishes*. With my second cocktail in one hand and her book in the other, I soon discovered the whole sordid tale of how Christian zealotry, political chicanery, and ruthless exploitation dropped the Hawaiian Islands into the laps of America's nineteenth-century conquistadores. Damn, just as I was starting to enjoy this place my social conscience kicks in!

Motivated, though reluctantly, to find Hawai'i's contemporary oppressors, I accepted an invitation from Derrick Kiyabu to visit MA'O Organic Farm on Oahu Island's west side. The drive took me past Honolulu's cheek-to-jowl ocean view condos and the Pearl Harbor Naval Base before the H1 Freeway deposited me onto Highway 93. This is the approximate place where the sign "Now Leaving Paradise, Welcome to Poverty" would be placed if tourist officials chose to acknowledge such things. But lacking most of what vacationers are looking for from a tropical getaway, the Wai'anae Coast, as it is commonly known, can only offer fast-food joints, scruffy commercial buildings, and rundown residential housing that rival third-world standards. I guess this is why the Lonely Planet guidebook refers to the region, almost quaintly, as "a little bit of Appalachia by the sea."

My pre-farm tour reached a crescendo when I happened by a homeless encampment cobbled together along a one-mile stretch of state beach. Late model cars—many rusted and in various states of disassembly—jerry-rigged shelters, and a mish mash of makeshift camping and cooking gear presented such a scene of destitution that even knuckle-dragging conservatives would advocate for immediate relief.

As I moved inland a couple of miles, the landscape and impressions changed. Small sections of dry, flat farmland intermingled with vast tracks of military land—securely fenced and sporting giant arrays of submarine-tracking sonar towers capable of detecting a flushing toilet in a Russian submarine north of Okinawa. It is here though, amid palm and banana trees, that you'll find the peaceful acres of MA'O Organic Farms, armed with nothing more dangerous than wholesome organic produce and forty or so eager farm interns between the ages of seventeen and twenty-four.

Like almost all the interns and staff, Derrick is wearing the farm's "No Panic, Go Organic" t-shirt. Noting some of the underlying principles of the program, he reminds me that "pre-contact" Hawaiians were 100 percent food self-reliant and that their traditional farming methods were totally organic. In a more pragmatic vein, he also explains the program's business model: "Organic produce generates the most revenue from our customers such as Whole Foods, numerous natural food stores, CSA members, and Honolulu's high-end restaurants." As a self-described social enterprise, the non-profit farm generates 40 percent of its million-dollar-plus annual budget from produce sales. This is how they support the youth development and leadership program that is at the core of the farm's mission. Promoting food security in the surrounding region is secondary to the need to generate funds for instructional costs, community college tuition, and stipends for the workers.

Without a doubt, the produce is top-notch. The packing sheds—two retrofitted chicken coops—are filled with interns washing and packing perfect heads of green and white bok choy, glowing red radishes, and gorgeous greens. A big whiteboard lists all the customers and the number of units each will purchase that day. As the young people pack each order in MA'O Farms custom boxes and load them on to the refrigerated delivery truck, the pride is evident in their smiles; after all, they grew it, picked it, and packed it. From the sales revenue, they'll be paid a monthly stipend by it. Moreover, the produce will help send them to college.

MA'O isn't just another scheme to reconnect kids to land, food, and a little income. According to Kamu Enos, MA'O's Social Entrepreneur Director, the farm is a training and leadership development program designed to overcome the poverty and social dysfunction that was so evident on my drive in. He tells me that "this region of Oahu has the highest concentration of native Hawaiians on all the Islands. We also have a 20 percent poverty rate, which is disproportionately higher for Hawaiians. Over 40 percent of our kids drop out of school and only 10 percent of our graduating high school class goes to college, and many of those leave during the first year." Derrick puts the problem more succinctly, "Our public education system has ripped off our kids."

When I noted the unusually high number of very heavy people I saw in Wai'anae, Kamu explained that, like other Native American communities, the ravages of the infamous "food" product, Spam, loss of land, and the decline of traditional practices have taken their toll on peoples' bodies as well as their souls. In what might be called the second wave of white man's disease (the first, as

Sarah Vowell makes clear, was the nineteenth-century smallpox and measles epidemics brought by missionaries and seamen that reduced the native Hawaiian population from 300,000 to 40,000), the American processed and fast-food diet and the paucity of fresh fruits and vegetables are degrading the community's health. "The root problem," said Kamu, "is the disconnect between our land, people, and economy. Instead [of controlling these things], we exist under the predatory practices of the military." Not only does the Defense Department control most of the land in the region, military recruiters find local Hawaiians easy targets for enlistment because good civilian job opportunities are so few.

Getting control of land, especially for farming, is a daunting challenge for Hawaiians—there's not much affordable, arable land that developers don't already have their mitts on. But sugar daddies do show up, and they are not always the kind that operated the cane plantations. In MA'O Organic Farms' case, the sweet guy is none other than Pierre Omidyar, founder of e-Bay. He generously dropped a cool million on the program, which, with assistance from the Trust for Public Land, bought the eleven acres that are now the heart of the farm.

Pua, who is twenty-one, is a MA'O youth leader and the first member of her family to go to college. She recently received her associate degree from Leeward Community College and is scheduled to start at the University of Hawai'i at Manoa in August. She tells me that high school didn't prepare her for college, but with her mother's encouragement and MA'O's help—counseling, remedial instruction, and peer support—she's climbed some pretty steep personal cliffs and is now ready for bigger challenges. While she's not likely to pursue farming as a career she credits the farm program with giving her the emotional tools she needed to succeed. "The farm experience is an inspiration. Like college, it's hard work. The farm grounds you because you have to manage your time, you have to work as a team with others to succeed, and you have to face the consequences of your actions."

For other young people like Pua, the path out of poverty starts with a walk down the farm's vegetable rows. Many start to eat better and lose weight. Kainoa is one youth worker who actually lost 130 pounds by exercising and changing his diet. But what the program cultivates even more than the farm's well composted soil is the interns' state of mind. Disempowered, brought up with low expectations, some homeless, they were staring at a future that promised little but a swift descent into diabetes and a life in the unemployment line. Now the steps out of poverty are more visible.

To grow and sell a half-million dollars of organic fruits and vegetables every year is no small feat. But to raise dozens of young leaders who can challenge the dominance of the condo kings and restore the economic and physical health of their people would no doubt bring a smile to the ancient kings and queens of Hawai'i.

CHAPTER EIGHT

Israel's War on Palestinian Olive Farmers

February, 2024

This is the only essay that looks at food injustices outside the US. But the connection to some notable American food projects and interests, as well as the current nature of the conflict, argued for its inclusion. Food and farming as political tools, economic development levers, and as a reflection of deep spiritual and cultural connection to the land are issues echoed in places across America. But on the West Bank and Gaza today, people are paying the price to retain those connections with their lives. Perhaps there is no place currently on earth where the threats to food sovereignty and security are higher. Biggest surprise: Even in the midst of poverty and a hostile military presence, high-quality food products can be produced and shipped to high-demand markets.

I grew up under the sway of Zionist ideology. Like a similar ideology that underpinned my 1950s and 1960s American history lessons, Zionism presented a virtuous cause framed by a tale of divine destiny that was forged in a cauldron of suffering and activated by a ferocious work ethic. My mother and father, who didn't have a Jewish bone in their bodies, raised me and my three siblings in a Presbyterian-lite manner. To highlight just how vanilla our religious life was, however, my mother would regale us with tales of the Jews making the deserts of their new Israeli nation bloom. She spared no details when sharing the emerging horrors of the Holocaust, and why the "chosen people" were entitled to every last acre of what was then called Palestine. Thusly imbued, I can remember joining in a burst of seventeen-year-old bravado that erupted from our high school cafeteria table in June of 1967 when we learned that Israel had "kicked the Arab's asses" in only six days.

But like our social studies textbooks that sometimes weren't worth the glue that bound them, the stories of messianic zeal that fired Zionism and, likewise, America's Manifest Destiny, had several pages "missing." Those were the unwritten chapters that would have told us of the trampling, enslavement, and near erasure of those who already occupied that land, as well as those people who were forced here after being separated from their traditional lands. Indeed, one humiliation imposed by the oppressor throughout history has been denying the vanquished access to their land, its fertility, and its productions. From the salting of seized fields in the ancient Middle East—"a covenantal curse, a means of ensuring desolation"—to the near annihilation of the buffalo by America's white settlers to today's apartheid wall in Palestine's West Bank, the conqueror not only cut the conquered off from their food and their livelihoods, they ensured their disappearance as a people.

Taking a page from those unwritten chapters, we see the same story unfold in the West Bank. The modern beginnings of that history go back seventy-five years to when the Zionists displaced hundreds of thousands of Palestinians from their traditional lands. It continued through Israel's seizure and occupation of the West Bank, and has now intensified since Hamas's barbaric attacks on Israeli sites on October 7, 2024.

According to Yesh Din, an Israeli human rights organization,

> October 7 was a launching pad for a campaign of incitement against Palestinians in the West Bank, focusing on farmers and on preventing the [olive] harvest ... False information that

Palestinian harvesters were out to attack [Israeli] settlers spread ... Israelis carried out planned attacks on people whose only sin was harvesting their own olives. [O]n October 28, 2023 a settler who was also a soldier on leave fatally shot Bilal Saleh, a father of four from a-Sawiyah. Bilal was harvesting olives with his children ... on his land in an area that does not require prior coordination with the military. The settler who killed Bilal was arrested and released five days later. (Yesh Din, n.d.)

Yesh Din, which is part of the non-profit New Israel Fund, has fastidiously documented the human rights violations of settlers and soldiers against Palestinians. Since October 7,389 Palestinians have been killed by Israel's military and civilian forces in the West Bank compared to twenty-nine Israelis killed (an additional 103 Palestinians were killed in the nine months before October 7). But a special form of intimidation was reserved for the olive harvest, which was at its peak this fall. The 2023 olive harvest season were marked by 113 incidents of violence against Palestinian harvesters, including soldiers and settlers physically assaulting harvesters (twenty-four incidents), firing live ammunition at harvesters (eleven incidents), and cutting down or torching 715 olive trees (twenty-nine incidents). Yesh Din concluded that the "scale of violence during the harvest was two to three times greater than in previous years." The incident reports and personal stories of the victims are reminiscent of the Ku Klux Klan's intimidation and harassment of Black Americans in the Jim Crow South, including the near total absence of prosecuting the offenders.

For Palestinians, olives are not just another crop that produces a vital stream of income, they are also a national and cultural symbol. According to the Palestinian Agriculture Relief Committee (PARC), there are an estimated 13 million olive trees in Palestine, some of whose roots go back 5,000 years, and whose ownership is spread across hundreds of thousands of smallholders. PARC (Agricultural Development Association, n.d.) diversified farming activities and overall respect make it the dominant Palestinian agricultural force. It oversees forty-one farmer co-ops that, in addition to olive growers, include producers of dates, almonds, poultry, and other crops. It also operates an agricultural training program for about 1,600 young people annually.

Robert Evert, a principal with the US-based fair trade organization Equal Exchange, tells me how inspiring his visits to PARC's training sites have been. "On the West Bank, people are getting beat up and shot at. In other words, there's not a lot of hope," he says. "But it's very moving to see the spirit of the young people in PARC's training program. It gives them hope and a reason to get up in the morning." Evert also adds that the young participants are very diverse with respect to gender, about 50/50 male and female.

As important as these organizing and training programs are, it's critical to the Palestinian economy that its agricultural products generate export revenue. That's where PARC's for-profit partner, Al-reef comes in. They've developed the capacity of producers to grow high-quality crops, and, with investment assistance from such groups as Oxfam, have constructed processing facilities such as a state-of-the-art olive oil bottling plant. The plant includes high-quality product testing and monitoring that are required to comply with the stringent "extra virgin" designation and export conditions to North American and European markets (as a purchaser of Al-reef's olive oil through Equal Exchange over the past three years, I can vouch for its quality and delicious flavor profile). For two months at harvest season, the olive oil presses are going 24/7. And there is no waste: olive pits are used to fuel the plant's boiler and the spent flesh is composted.

Saleem Abu Ghazaleh is Al-reef's general manager. As such, he oversees the farmer connections, processing, marketing, and shipping of their products. Though a successful professional who now runs one of the more substantial non-governmental enterprises in the West Bank, Saleem "enjoyed" a youthful Palestinian rite of passage by resisting the Israeli occupation and paying the price: five years in prison. Rob Evert has spent time with Saleem at his Al-reef facilities in Ramallah. This included time in his office which, according to Evert, is tiny. "Saleem told me that his office is about the same size as his prison cell, but then he said, 'at least I now have a key!'"

In a February 11th correspondence with me and Equal Exchange, Saleem said, "the level of violence committed by Israeli settlers and Israel forces has not been slowing in the West Bank, on the contrary, they have been increasing. The leaders of those settlers who are also Ministers in this right-wing Israeli government ...

call for the expulsion of Palestinians from Gaza or the West Bank." Citing the many hostile actions and restrictions on farmers as well as unusually poor growing conditions in 2023, he said the supply of Palestinian olive oil is way down. The decline in supply was also due to the loss of 3,000 tons of olive oil in the Gaza Strip because the war there prevented the 2023 harvest from taking place. "We had to decrease Equal Exchange's order of olive oil because of the situation of farmers," Saleem said. Equal Exchange normally buys about 25,000 bottles of olive oil annually, about 15 percent of Al-reef's production. While the supply cut will be a small inconvenience for Equal Exchange's shoppers, the lost sales is potentially devastating for Palestinians.

There is a pall of oppression hanging over the West Bank and Gaza the likes of which would never be tolerated in the United States. According to a recent *New York Times Magazine* article (Wells, 2024), the per capita income in the West Bank is $5,600 compared to $50,000 in many of the illegal Israeli settlements. Economic prospects, always bleak at best, were made worse when Israel suspended payments to the Palestinian Authority, and West Bank Palestinians could no longer go into Israel to work. This adversely affected 139,000 Palestinian workers (according to Saleem, the loss of paychecks forced some olive oil co-ops to sell their oil early simply to raise cash for their members' basic living expenses). Israel routinely tears down Palestinian buildings, both residential and agricultural, including 15,000 homes in Jerusalem, supposedly because they lacked building permits. Politically, the Palestinians have never consented to be governed by Israel, yet they live under an anti-democratic, apartheid occupation. In light of these conditions, is it any wonder that there are periodic intifadas and, sadly, it is why many Palestinians regard October 7 as their liberation day, "the day when they became visible again."

Almost a year ago, I attended a lecture by Miko Peled who wrote a book called *The General's Son: Journey of an Israeli in Palestine*. His father was a prominent military leader in Israel's 1948 and 1967 wars, which enhances Peled's credibility as an outspoken critic of Israel's occupation of Palestine. Speaking forcefully, he ticks off a litany of Israel's abuses asserting that they constitute crimes against humanity, ethnic cleansing, and even genocide. He asks the audience, "how could people who survived the Holocaust do these things?" Perhaps with my age group in mind, Peled urges us not to think of Israel's illegal settlements as the idealized "hippie" kibbutz of our youth (to impress the Jewish woman I was dating in college, I may have even suggested joining one). These are now the large settlements of evangelical Jews, supplied with thousands of weapons by the IDF, and terrorizing West Bank Palestinians. Peled called upon the audience as American taxpayers to make a moral decision to hold our own government accountable for funding these crimes. Lastly, he warned us not to be put off by accusations of anti-Semitism, a default term that is now used to shield Israel from criticism.

All recommendations for peace, reconciliation, or the much-touted two-state solution feel hopelessly faraway in today's climate of hate. As Mohammad Shtayyeh, the Palestinian prime minister, put it, "Israel ... is behaving like a wounded bull. They're acting in a mood of revenge, killing for the sake of killing." Suggesting that the bull do anything other than exhaust its blood lust feels hopeless for now. Yet the taking of land, the uprooting of trees whose millenniums of witness take in Jesus, Abraham, and Muhammad; taking the harvest from the community and the fruits of labor from the farmer, these are forms of retribution reserved for those who not only deny the existence of others, but also deny their own humanity and humanity's common bond with the earth. To thwart such blindness requires the light of hope and witness provided by Yesh Din, PARC, Al-reef, and other forward-looking, on the ground organizations willing to risk their money, their energy and sometimes their lives for a brighter future. And it requires American political leaders with real courage to end the bloodshed and forge a path to peace and prosperity.

Update: Neither Palestinian dates nor olive oil are available through Equal Exchange as of this writing. The conflict has substantially reduced the production and processing capacity of Palestinian farmer co-ops and Al-reef.

PART TWO
People

CHAPTER NINE

A Rainbow of Farmers

March, 2015

In early 2015, inspired and disheartened by police brutality directed against people of color, I wrote two pieces on the role of race in the American food system by focusing on three Black leaders. The following combines and edits those two original pieces to highlight, once again, the role that race plays in what feels at times like an endless and frustrating search for justice. Within the context of the food movement, one manifestation of that search—a glimmer of hope in a larger context of racial struggles—is the growth of participation and the evolution of leadership among people of color. Biggest surprise: The rise of young Black farmers.

It doesn't matter if you don't want to be a part of America's race story—it has a way of finding you. This came home to me recently during my morning practice of reading poetry, the purpose of which is to warm up gently to a wobbly world. Picking up from where I'd left the book marker the previous day, the first poem that gave itself to me was Audre Lorde's 1978 "Power" whose first lines, "A policeman who shot down a ten year old in Queens/stood over the boy with his cop shoes in childish blood" couldn't have hit me harder if it was a baseball bat.

Astonishingly, I read this poem two days after the NYC decision to not indict the policeman responsible for the choke-hold death of Eric Garner. Whether it's 1978 in Queens or 2014 in Staten Island, criminal acts by those we pay to protect us confound our sensibilities, make us feel powerless in the face of power, and evoke the all-too-human urge to retaliate. The never-ending story of American racism screams at us to do something, anything, to relieve the anguish.

But what? Choosing to act non-violently will always be my modus operandi. Yes, I can march, I can shout, I can commit (and have committed) acts of civil disobedience, but as I started doing forty-four years ago, changing the food system will always be my battleground in the war on injustice and racism. Near the end of my first book *Closing the Food Gap* I said that, "As a person of privilege and power whose professional agenda has been to reduce the ill effects of the food system on people who bear little resemblance to myself, I have become intensely aware of what I can and cannot do."

In other words, food justice will not be attained solely through the efforts of well-intentioned white guys, no matter how good their work. Achieving food security, access to healthy and affordable food, and social and economic equity for all will only be achieved when a significant share of the movement's leadership is assumed by those with a greater personal stake in the outcome, i.e., people of color.

To that end let me share a few words about some inspiring African-American food system leaders with whom I've had the privilege to work.

Rashid Nuri and Truly Living Well Farm

"I used to protest, but now I build the future." That was how Rashid Nuri, CEO of the Atlanta-based Truly Living Well (TLW) urban farm (Truly Living Well, n.d.) sized up his role in response to the Ferguson and Staten Island verdicts. Gazing over several acres of highly productive December vegetable plots, it was obvious that Rashid was building a very viable future. As we have all been reminded time and again, the world's population is becoming increasingly urbanized. The effective use of undeveloped urban and peri-urban land for food production will no longer be considered a nicety but a necessity.

The kale, collards, onions, and broccoli were vigorous and awaiting their turn for future harvests that will be sold at TLW's farm stand, their community-supported agriculture project, and area restaurants. Located barely 100 yards from Interstate 85's eight lanes of rip-roaring traffic, and just a few blocks from the peaceful oasis of the Reverend Martin Luther King, Jr. Historic Site, the farm also serves as a highly visible demonstration site for numerous food, farm, and sustainability initiatives. An aquaponic greenhouse, a state of the art "rocket heated" greenhouse, a model, large-scale composting site, and too many varieties of fruit trees and berry bushes to keep track of sprout from what used to a public housing site. This alternative urban landscape is the fruition of Rashid's vision and leadership, and, just as importantly, a powerful model for a robust urban agriculture presence that embraces the diversity of its place and people.

Kwabena Nkromo and the Georgia Food Policy Council

Food and agriculture policy is a murky area often overwhelmed by special interests and more money than principles. As subject matter goes, it's often so dense that a bucket of it can stop a bullet fired at close range. But neither of these factors has deterred Kwabena Nkromo from taking the reins of the Georgia Food Policy Council (GFPC), a statewide organization founded in 2012 that has set its sights on the numerous food and farm challenges facing Georgia's citizens.

Both policy work and leadership are natural evolutions for Kwabena, who has played a major role in the social enterprise organization Atlanta Food & Farm, LLC. Organized as a social benefit corporation, Atlanta Food and Farm serves a growing niche as a consulting group for community food systems planning and urban agriculture development.

Though still a "newbie" in the food policy world (GPFC's website is currently under reconstruction), the Council is moving ahead with the formation of a Georgia Farmers Market Association, and sees itself working with such partners as Georgia Organics and the Georgia Food Oasis for better policies from farm to plate. According to Kwabena, "These efforts will not only be focused on the Georgia General Assembly and other legislative bodies, but also through the influence of actions and choices each of us make as food citizens."

Natasha Bowen and *The Color of Food*

For those of us who still think that food is grown exclusively by fifty-nine-year-old white men wearing freshly laundered overalls and John Deere caps, photo-journalist Natasha Bowen's book *The Color of Food* (Bowens, 2015) may come as a shock. In what can only be described as the classic existential American road trip, Bowens takes us from coast to coast in her trusty automobile "Lucille" in search of roots, farmers of color, and truths hidden in plain sight. Along the way we meet African-American, Latino, Native American, and Asian farmers—not a single one of whom fits any agricultural stereotype known to me.

It's a story that begins with a young woman of interracial heritage plunging her hands into the soil of a place where she found connection and community. Bowens could have stayed among her fellow communards, or, as she put it, "back-to-the-land hipsters" honing her farming skills and adding to the growing bounty of locally produced food. But she chose instead to trade in the dirt 'neath her nails for a laptop and camera to weave together stories about farmers of color. Her choice will no doubt inspire other young people to respond to their own inner agrarian.

The Color of Food is one of those well-written picture books that works at many levels. It is certainly America's race story etched across a roughly textured agricultural landscape, where the oppression of 400 years finds contemporary expression. It's also a tale of Bowens herself, who uses her camera lens to find her way through the lens of a conflicted past to a more hopeful future. It's the story of places lost and places found, and how people ripped from their native lands have rediscovered their identities in new communities. And, without a doubt, it's a tale of the suffocating blanket of the industrial food system and its uncanny ability to suck the life from our souls.

One of Bowens's gifts to us is Daniel Whitaker, a Black ninety-three-year-old retired hog farmer from North Carolina, who gives a verbatim account of the medieval practice of sharecropping. "We would make ten cents a day ... but that was the way it was," he tells us. "Your parents would work all the year and the opposite people [his almost childlike term for white people] would ... tell you, 'you didn't earn any money this year.' Those things rested hard on my mind ....I knew I wanted to do something different." And he did just that, clawing his way to the purchase of 314 acres of land where he successfully raised hogs and grew peaches, apples, pears, and corn. Mr. Whitaker passed in 2014.

Fortunately, Bowens is not one of those writers eager to erect a pedestal before she knows who to put on it. She grasps her subjects intuitively and renders them in loving but carefully constructed frames. Her photographic images are strong, and she grants her subjects ample space to tell their stories in their own words. Bowen's commentary provides just enough connective tissue to maintain an even narrative flow, and enough context so that we can easily see the big picture.

And, of course, there's never any doubt which way Bowens's compass needle points. Leading us into the future with the book's final chapter, "Generation Rising," Bowens issues what might be read as her generation's agroecological manifesto: "We refuse to settle for anything less than transformation and what we think is just. My hope is that this willpower ... will truly revolutionize not only the food system, but the way we live on this planet."

We see the embodiment of that will in the struggle of young, landless farmers of color Christina and Tahz Rivera-Chapman of Tierra Negra Farms. Experimenting with different forms of farming on various parcels of borrowed land, they cobble together a livelihood from off-farm jobs to sustain their burning desire to farm full time. Their frustration and growing rage become palpable when Christina speaks of trying to work "within the framework of money and capitalism—which we know is explicitly trying to screw one group over another." But their frustrations with a system that doesn't help beginning farmers has led them to an alternative plan to secure communally owned farmland. Their dream is to work with several young farmers of color to collectively pursue common agricultural goals while also forging bonds between generations of farmers.

Though I believe that a healthy dose of subjectivity is sometimes necessary to ensure a writer's objectivity, I did find myself bridling at times over Bowens's repetitious exuberance. Her too-frequent descents into diatribe as well as overstated assertions unrestrained by facts did leave me huffing and puffing on more than one occasion. But over time, I am sure, Bowens will learn to trust her pen and pictures sufficiently to let the reader find their own conclusions. In the meantime, one would have hoped that a strong editor might have curtailed the author's excesses.

That being said, I will put aside my critic's hat to state that we must listen to authentic rage, even when it is not filtered by analysis or supported by citations. It's not always the absolute truth or the reliability of the data that matters, but the sense of truth as expressed by the speaker. Bowens courageously wades into territory that is heavily mined with emotion and scarred by some of the worst abuses in North American history. She should be praised for revealing the grace and resilience of the wounded and their children and the children of their children.

I found myself wondering out loud why, in the face of unrelenting oppression, *The Color of Food* characters didn't either run, or, running out of patience, stand and fight what would have been a suicidal battle. The only answer that makes sense to me is that the roots of farming go so deep into the land that they draw on enormous reservoirs of strength, and that the love of place is an instinct that can buffer us against the worst impulses of revenge. Bowens' stories are first and foremost a triumph of humanity over racism, and a victory, related through numerous tales of pain and struggle, that we the alienated nomads of the twenty-first century might well heed.

Where Do We Go From Here?

Circling back to the racism-inspired carnage that exacts such a heavy toll on the American soul, it's worth asking if this nation's food movement can't take more concrete steps to stem "the blood-dimmed tide?" In 2010, 55 percent of shooting homicide victims were Black people even though they only make up 13 percent of the US population. While people of color are far and away the highest percentage of victims of food and farm injustices, it is reasonable to say, even without the benefit of accurate data, that they are inadequately represented in leadership roles with groups attempting to address those injustices.

Again, what I said in *Closing the Food Gap* makes more sense now than when I wrote it in 2007: "As I use the talents God gave me ... to make the lives of others at least a little better, I will ... make way for, and get out of the way of those whose voices more genuinely call out for change than mine ever can." It feels as if that time has come; I can be an ally, a teacher, a trainer, a donor, and a comrade-in-arms. But if the body count is to stop growing, and if "food justice for all" will no longer be "a dream deferred," then the leadership of the food movement must do more to show its colors.

CHAPTER TEN

I Have Seen the Future of Medicine: It Is Dr. Yum

June, 2014

I found the pediatrician, Dr. Nimali Fernando, quite by accident one spring day while researching food projects in central Virginia. After only thirty minutes of interviewing her, I knew that I had stumbled upon a medical professional who embodied every quality of a positive health care provider that I ever imagined was possible. Beyond a style and a practice that was perfectly suited for a period when our diet-related illnesses were going through the roof, Dr. Fernando exhibited a blend of entrepreneurism, imagination, and leadership second to none. To summarize a model career devoted to social and individual change, my prescription is: master your chosen profession and its basic skill sets (minimum ten years); develop an innovation or specialty, refine it, demonstrate its effectiveness, disseminate it (minimum ten years); create or join an entity that will then take it nationwide. That's Nimali Fernando in a nutshell. Biggest surprise: See the update.

As a newly minted medical doctor, Nimali Fernando's baptism by fire came in a Houston community pediatric clinic where she would see as many as sixty new-born babies a day. Long hours and a bone-crushing caseload that never gave her more than fifteen minutes to spend with a patient took their toll. But it was the high prevalence of overweight and obese children that fanned the flames of her growing frustration with the way pediatric medicine was practiced in this country, a frustration that would soon sow the seeds for a new vision of medicine.

It would take nine more years in a traditional pediatrics practice before those seeds would sprout. During that time Dr. Fernando paid her dues by performing the requisite number of immunizations and treating more ear aches than any doctor should have to in a lifetime. She also continued to see her share of the 30 percent of children nationally who are overweight and obese. But it was the other 70 percent that began to seize her attention. The majority of these children, while not showing weight problems, had symptoms that were clearly linked to poor eating behaviors, including parents who simply didn't know how to cook.

Dr. Fernando realized she was chained to a treatment treadmill that would never get her any closer to the root causes of her patients' illnesses; that no matter how many hours she'd put in or prescriptions she'd write, nothing would change. It was then that she checked on those seeds that were now becoming vigorous plants, and decided the time was right to shed her white coat and the trappings of a conventional doctor's office. And like a butterfly free of its cocoon, Dr. Fernando stretched her wings and morphed into Dr. Yum, food and health crusader par excellence!

Opened in 2012, Yum Pediatrics and its non-profit arm, The Dr. Yum Project (Dr. Yum Project, n.d.) is located in an unassuming central Virginia office park. Curiously, its neighbors include a Burger King, Giant Supermarket, and the county office of the Virginia Farm Bureau. But step inside and no matter how sick you feel, the cheery food- and garden-themed interior will brighten your spirits. There's comfy, children-sized furniture, plastic fruit and veggie toys, a wide-screen TV on the wall with appropriate cooking shows running on a continuous loop, all set against a soft, pastel color scheme of pea green, carrot orange, and blueberry blue. And if you're still not sure what Dr. Yum's message is, the poster-size Michael Pollan quote on the wall—"Eat Food, Not Too Much, Mostly Plants"—should clue you in.

The office was not open to patients on the Saturday morning Dr. Fernando showed me around, which was part of the reason she was wearing running shorts and a dirty pink t-shirt emblazoned with the word "Compost." She apologized for her admittedly grimy appearance, telling me that she, her husband, and two young boys had just completed a two-and-half mile community mud run. Showing me around the examination rooms—"Pea Room," "Carrot Room"—it was easy to see how children (to say nothing of anxious parents) would feel comfortable amidst the uncluttered environment that exuded warmth rather than sterility, beautiful graphics of fruits and vegetables rather than wall charts of body parts, and traditional Sri Lankan tapestries representing Dr. Fernando's heritage. All manner of traditional pediatric medicine, including pediatric gynecology are practiced in this space, but the "treatment modality" that receives the most attention is eating.

That is why the largest room in the office—and the center of her practice—is the Dr. Yum teaching kitchen where the road to wellness begins for many. It is in this spacious, well-outfitted modern kitchen where Dr. Fernando and her associates teach cooking, eating, and tasting. If you have children, you know that it is the tasting that matters, which is why she has assembled an esteemed panel of "experts"—twenty-four taste testers whose ages range from one to thirteen. Using recipes for healthy food, e.g., the crunchy apple sandwich—two apple slices, unsweetened whole grain cereal, and sunflower butter—Dr. Fernando shares her creations with her young experts who report their reaction on Dr. Yum's five-level rating scale: Super Yuck, Yuck, OK, Yum, or Super Yum, each one with its own happy/unhappy face emoticon.

Cooking classes are taught with children under six years old and their parents together, but with children seven to twelve, no parents are present. Dr. Fernando has found that mom or dad's participation creates a weird dynamic that tends to reduce the child's ability to learn. To teach how one can prepare and enjoy a healthy breakfast, she hosts a pajama party cooking class for kids who, of course, show up in their PJs. She has also developed her own food curriculum which is being piloted with a number of area teachers and about 200 children. As one teacher put it, "We can't believe how the Dr. Yum curriculum has changed the way our kids eat!"

There's also a garden, and not the usual Wal-Mart pot with a couple of scraggly cherry tomatoes struggling for life. The 900-square feet, fenced-in growing space attached to the end of the Yum Pediatric building will be going into full production this year. Robust tomatoes, however, were already growing from a dozen 5-gallon tubs, a peach tree was displaying its first marble-size fruit, and old rain boots had been repurposed as marigold pots.

Taking in this scene where the combined footprint of Dr. Yum's kitchen, teaching space, and garden exceed that of the square footage devoted to treatment and administration, I couldn't help but devise a ratio—call it the Winne Wellness Index—that might have implications for how we address health care in this country. This is best expressed as the combined space of gardens (G), kitchens (K), and food education (E) (feel free to substitute dollars, hours, or healthy breakfast pajama parties) divided by the combined space of treatment (T) and administration (A) (dollars, hospital beds, or rip-off health insurance companies are also suitable metrics).

I can imagine that this relationship could be expressed mathematically as:

$$\frac{G \pm K \pm E}{T + A} =$$ (When the ratio is 1 or greater, the country's overall health is high)

Because we in the US spend more on health care than any other nation, and generally are sicker than any of the seventeen most developed nations, we have to ask ourselves how we've got it so wrong. A big part of the problem is that our health policies and agriculture policies are as distant from one another as Mars is from Venus. Based on these obvious disparities, one can imagine that if the Winne Wellness Index was applied to the US, the ratio would be something like 0.0000016, or only slightly higher than the lifespan of a ripe cantaloupe. With a few thousand more Dr. Yums practicing pediatrics, supported by communities and schools that share Dr. Nimali Fernando's theory of health, that ratio might one day begin to soar skyward. That would be Yummy!

Update: After a highly successful ten-year run, Nimali Fernando closed her practice in 2023 to focus her attention on the non-profit Dr. Yum Project, now known as Touchpoints. As Dr. Fernando put it, "Touchpoints [will] help pediatricians nationwide with the overwhelming challenges of addressing childhood obesity." Her goal is "to have partner pediatricians and preschool programs ... in all fifty states." Her former clinic building is being reopened as a wellness center.

CHAPTER ELEVEN

It's Not Easy Being a Commercial Egg Farmer

September, 2020 and September, 2022

Farming is a fearsome enterprise. Even when prodigiously hard work turns into profits, the mental and emotional tolls it takes on the farmer and family force even the toughest of souls to ask, "Why bother?" For the 98 percent of us who are not farmers, the task is first to understand the sometimes-brutal realities of producing local food, including the financial investment, and then to do all things possible—policy, personal, and community—to mitigate the hardships and reduce gaps between producer and consumer. It is one of those social and economic divides that can be healed. Biggest surprise: The durability and resilience of a person committed to farming.

Part One: Dogs and COVID-19

First off, I'm not sure if Randy Cruz's Cruz Ranch in Sapello, New Mexico is the region's biggest egg producer. Clawing my way through USDA's 2017 Agriculture Statistics seems to suggest that out of the state's 2,848 farms that reported raising poultry, the Cruz Ranch was easily in the top ten. What I do know is that turning seventy hilly acres in Northern New Mexico into a commercial egg-laying operation was an uphill climb requiring love, intelligence, and money. What I also learned is that staying in business takes blood, guts, and more money.

 Take the night in early October last year when there *were* about 2,700 laying hens and an assortment of ducks, turkeys, geese, and peacocks tucked safely into their coops when Randy went to bed. When he woke the next morning, the number of birds had plummeted to 1,500. The scene that greeted him was one of carnage as nearly 1,200 birds lay dead and dismembered about the coops and yard. He didn't need to gather any forensic evidence to determine that this was not the work of coyotes. The nonsensical killing had been committed by his neighbor's four German shepherds that had tunneled under the yard's fence.

 The Cruz Ranch story started five years ago when Randy and his then-partner and now husband, Dan, decided to return from their home in Palm Springs, California to start a farm in Northern New Mexico. Randy had been raised on a 6,000-acre ranch in nearby Gascan as part of his family's third generation in the same house. There, he developed a love/hate relationship with the region that is known for its stunning beauty and agrarian lifestyle, but offers little opportunity. "My mother divorced my father who was the town drunk," Randy tells me. "We then moved to Oregon which was the best thing that ever happened to us. If I had stayed, I would've become a drunk or a loser."

 Randy, who is sixty, uses disarming candor to explain why he chose to take up farming, which was not a part of his upbringing. "I needed something to do that used up my energy and was fun," he said. Since he's constantly in motion, it's obvious why he chose something as physical as farming. But making the leap from a comfortable California lifestyle to a farming life in New Mexico's mountains, even when you have roots there, is a big one. Initially unfamiliar with commercial poultry methods, Randy learned everything possible about eggs, chickens, and birds that quack and gobble from books he'd read late into the night. Starting out with 100 chickens, he quickly lost forty-five to neighbors' dogs and coyotes. He ordered 300 more chickens, reinforced his fences, and added a couple of border collies to perform security and herding duties.

With hundreds of chickens each laying an egg a day, ducks a little less, and turkeys one every two days, Randy soon had the supply he needed to meet the demand generated by a growing list of loyal customers. Restaurants in and around Santa Fe, Cid's Food Market in Taos, the Dixon Food Co-op, and three farmers' markets comprised the largest portion of his customer base. While his eggs weren't certified USDA organic, most of his chicken feed was and his birds were running free and easy under the New Mexico sun in a generously-sized yard planted in cover crops. Things were hectic, Randy was hustling and happy, especially after a farmers' market when he brought home a bundle of cash.

There's another part of Randy's start-up story that also requires mention. He wasn't a young hippie who lived out of the back of a van trying to make a go of farming with some borrowed parental bucks and a used rototiller. Randy and Dan had been sufficiently successful in business in California to buy the Sapello property, a former religious retreat center, without going into debt. They also drew on their own resources for working capital. "It takes five to seven months of feed, water, heat lamps, and hard, caring work before a chicken lays a single egg," Randy tells me, noting that $13,000 in feed alone is required to fill his three grain bins. Even when the first eggs finally appear, they are generally too small for commercial sale, so Randy donates them to the Bienvenidos Outreach Food Pantry.

A sufficient supply of start-up capital, however, doesn't insulate you from the misfortunes of farming. When I learned of Randy's chicken slaughter, I asked him if he was going to have the dogs put down and seek restitution from their owners. He said no, "I have to live with these neighbors, and full restitution for my losses would break them." But he soon discovered that his charitable impulses had limits. Three weeks later, the same German shepherds returned, and this time Randy caught them in the act. After they killed thirty-four turkeys, six peacocks, and 125 pullets, Randy shot three of the marauding dogs. His patience exhausted; he filed a lawsuit against their owner.

"It was a real awful thing," he told me over the phone. "The dogs were looking back at me when I had cornered them in the barn as if to say, 'it's not our fault, we're just dogs; it's our owner's fault.' I hated to do it." His pain was palpable, and his reluctance to escalate the conflict with his neighbor was evident. But he felt there was no other way if he wanted to stay in business.

COVID-19

In a twist of Old Testament fury, the coronavirus swept into New Mexico upending the state's food system applecart. While one might expect that this unforeseen event likened Randy to Job—chickens smote by dogs, a plague upon his people—something different occurred. Suddenly demand for locally grown food went through the roof. "Egg sales are out of control," he told me in late March. People were suddenly making hour-and-a-half drives to his farm from Santa Fe to buy a case of eggs (135). Randy said, "It's nice that people are coming to my farm; they've never done that before."

Even though his three regular farmers' markets keep him busy, Randy's received requests from the Santa Fe Farmers' Market to sell there. He's lost his restaurant sales due to the virus, but he can sell everything he produces now to Cid's. But this is when one injustice closes a door at the same time another one opens. Randy's egg supply is well down because he's still recovering from the great fall poultry massacre. "Cid's wants to buy sixteen to eighteen cases a week, but I can only produce enough now to sell them six." In other words, the coronavirus has created demand for Randy's egg that he can't fulfill until the replacement birds are fully producing.

Randy Cruz is a resilient and commercially viable farmer. But the threats are always lurking, sometimes from as close as next door, and other times from across the globe. Your chances of survival are enhanced if you can draw on a reservoir of working capital to weather farming's uncertainties. Therein lies a lesson for today's foodies: either we as a community underwrite the risk that our local farmers face—in other words, *we* become their insurance policy—or we rely on well-financed forms of corporate agriculture. Summing up the challenges, Randy said, "If I was poor, I would've been shattered long ago. You need deep pockets to be independent and operate, even at my modest scale."

Part Two: Two Years Later—Fire and Flood

A vulture is circling overhead as I'm staring at the rubble of a house that used to be a home. Randy Cruz, the sad owner of these ruins, is giving me a tour of this ungodly collection of charred debris. "There's my bed," he says, pointing to the remnants of a bedspring. "Under that is where I kept my guns, but I can't find them. They must have melted." A stack of red, yellow, and orange Fiesta tableware sits where the kitchen used to be, covered in soot but still neatly stacked, the only stroke of color to relieve an otherwise blackened scene of total devastation. Asking him if I could take a photo, Randy poses in front of a small woodstove, one of the few recognizable items amidst the twisted sheet metal and piles of brick. "Sure," he says chuckling, "Should I start a fire?" Fortunately, three months after one of New Mexico's worst wildfires in history, his sense of humor is still intact.

Any reasonable person—even natural risk takers, like farmers—would assume that catastrophes like rampaging dogs and a pandemic in just the last two years was more than your fair share. But this spring, just two years after the lockdown began, smoke was blowing from the direction of Hermit's Peak across Randy's farm. Pretty soon firefighters were everywhere, evacuation orders were issued, and the flames swept through Randy's farm on their way to consuming 350,000 acres of New Mexico's forests and grasslands. But just as the final embers of the house he shared with his husband Dan had died out, the angry gods of the Pecos Wilderness whipped up a gully-womper of a monsoon deluge that drowned pastures, moved fences into the next county, and turned roads into canals only fit for amphibious vehicles. Every farmer knows that shit happens, but these events were beyond excremental.

If there was any justice left in the universe, Randy was certainly due some. Though the wildfire took out his home, it spared the chicken coops (900 baby chickens were lost to the April cold because power was lost for weeks and his heaters couldn't operate), two other houses on his property, and most of his farm equipment. The mercurial behavior of the fire was apparent everywhere. A bone-jarring ride in Randy's ATV throughout the Manuelitas Creek area and along county road A4A revealed house after house burned to the ground interspersed with a house that was untouched. Hillsides and ridgelines were nothing but blackened pegs of needleless ponderosas that would alternate with pastures later made verdant by the floods.

A bumpy ride down a washed-out road may not be the best place to administer trauma therapy, but I asked Randy how he feels about all this, and if he ever thinks about giving up farming. "All I know is that I got a business to run," he replies. "I don't think about giving up; I just keep going." One can argue about forms of denial and stages of grief, but you can't help but wonder about farmers who are unable to take time to heal because they have a hundred chores to do. Maybe community support helps, which came from Randy's many neighbors who volunteered to collect eggs because his workers were forced to leave. And maybe some fleeting moments of care come from the loyal farmers' market customers who lined up at Randy's stall on May 20th to welcome him back with hugs and kind words. One might hope, however, that there was more than good wishes and FEMA bucks to shore up our farmers' resilience. Sometimes mending souls is just as important as mending fences.

Persistence, capital, faith, and deep wells of human energy may buffer farming's fraught enterprise. No matter how favorably the gods look down upon you from season to season, or how many resources you have to deflect the slings and arrows, it's always three steps forward, two steps back, one year, two steps forward and three steps back the next. If over a lifetime you come out a little bit ahead, then you've done well. In the meantime, tending to the well-being of those who voluntarily choose that struggle—to feed us, among other reasons—is a community job. To simply praise farmers for their endurance and tenacity in the face of so much hardship is not enough. We better be there—emotionally as well as financially—when they need help, even when they don't ask for it.

Update: Randy's husband passed away in 2023. Thanks in part to some sizeable FEMA checks for the fire damage, Randy has been able to rebuild and restore his lost buildings and damage to his property. He's raising more chickens and selling more eggs than ever and has diversified his farm into vegetable production. The hills and forests around his farm still show the fire and flood damage.

CHAPTER TWELVE

My Dinner with Embry

June, 2022

One common by-product of imagination is joy, a feeling—more precisely a human characteristic—that many highly creative people give off as abundantly as solar rays fall to the earth. When that quality is also combined with the pursuit of justice, that arduous and sometimes violent task is lightened, fitted with wings, and capable of disarming the most ardent of opponents. Great leaders and teachers often possess these capabilities, and when focused on injustices, become powerful forces for change. Biggest surprise: The African Sankofa bird is capable of looking backward and forward at the same time.

The ineffable Jim Embry, raconteur and food activist extraordinaire, motored through Santa Fe early this June as part of his Kentucky to Hawaiʻi "Joy and Justice Journey." I convinced him to join me at my favorite local eatery, The Shed, for a margarita and chili-laden enchilada. The deal was simple, I pick up the tab in return for an hour of his thoughts. Three hours later, there was no doubt I came out ahead.

Up until he retired a few years ago, Jim was the Director of Community Education for the University of Kentucky Cooperative Extension where he worked with county agents on urban agriculture and community food projects across the state. He's also part of an extended and diverse family farming enterprise. Wearing both hats—an African-American farmer and University educator—Jim has engaged with USDA over the ongoing anti-discrimination Pickford case. He tells me,

> Our family has a history of interaction with USDA over the last ten years. The county people from USDA just hem and haw every time you ask for help. The good old boy network is alive and well in my county! But on the other hand, African-American farmers haven't taken advantage of USDA loan programs. Much of that is due to generational trauma. I hear from farmers "my grandfather was messed over by USDA, and, hey, I'm not going there."

Mark: Every time I encounter someone who was a victim of racism, I'm always surprised that more people don't turn violent. Instead, they find a way to navigate peacefully through the hostility of others and the pain of their own anger.

Jim: It's amazing! That shit should be written up in psychology books for courses 101 to 501!

Mark: But before we wade into this more, you have an important decision to make: do you want green or red chili?

Jim: Christmas.

Mark: Whoa! You must be a native! So, when did your life of activism begin?

Jim: I've been active since I was ten years old because my mother was the state president of the Congress of Racial Equality [CORE] and we spent a lot of time on the picket lines. I became president of the north Kentucky youth chapter of the NAACP, and eventually statewide president.

Mark: Obviously, your mother influenced you, but why have you chosen both civil rights and food work as lifetime pursuits?

Jim: My mother's grandparents were enslaved. My mother and her parents had to give up their bus seats in the 1930s and 40s. My family's culture was to protest these things; on the picket line, I was used to getting cussed out and spit on.

Mark: Navigating your way through such horrors without responding violently requires the skills of a saint. How did you do it?

Jim: One of my three great-grandfathers who fought on the Union side in the Civil War died at a battle in Kentucky. He left behind his wife and seven children, all about two years apart. What was my great-grandmother going to do? She was living in a county that had confederate sympathies. But she found her way through those challenges by holding her tongue and not allowing her demeanor to antagonize white people. All seven kids were inspired by their mother and they all eventually owned their own small farms.

Mark: Last summer, I drove from Santa Fe to Connecticut and back again making several stops along the way to gather up community food stories. You are doing the same thing, except that you're going from Kentucky to California, and on to Hawai'i, then home again. I called my trip a "Voyage of Discovery," and you are calling yours "The Joy and Justice Journey." In these divisive times, joy and justice aren't two words I hear juxtaposed very often. Why joy and justice, and maybe more importantly—I'm seventy-two and you're seventy-three—what's driving old guys like us to do this much driving?

Jim: My short answer is I don't know any better! A longer version is that the tour is simply a continuation of my family's social justice/social change journey—this year's manifestation. In reality, I've actually been traveling for a long, long time!

Mark: Yes, you are kind of an itinerant preacher ...

Jim: We were reared in the Black Baptist Church, which had many gatherings all over the state. They always had lots of food and prayer. Because my father worked on the railroad, we got free train passes that allowed us to travel and visit family.

With Slow Food, I got to go to Tierra Madre 2008 because of my role in co-founding the Lexington Food Co-op in 1972 [the "Lex Food Co-op" is a multi-faceted and beautiful grocery store that I had the pleasure of visiting several years ago] on principles that align well with Slow Food's—work with food that is local, healthy, and organic. Slow Food is about food that is good, clean, and fair. Similar principles. But there's another reason as well. When my Aunt Bessie wondered why I was going to Italy, she asked me, "what's slow food?" I said, "Aunt Bessie, it's what you've been doing your whole life."

Mark: But how did the notion of joy become kissing cousins with justice?

Jim: Slow Food USA asked me to be the primary writer of their Equity, Inclusion, and Justice Manifesto. But there was a push back around some of the language. I wanted social justice to be woven into everything at Slow Food. We started a campaign to get the manifesto out to all the chapters. So rather than calling it something contentious like the "Dismantling Racism Manifesto" or the "Anti White Supremacy" campaign, we decided to call it the "Joy and Justice Campaign."

Mark: That's fascinating. I came into the food movement in my teens. I was in college and raising money for famine relief in Africa. I saw food as the gateway to social change. I started a co-op; started a breakfast program. Yes, it was social justice work, but too often we were forced to sacrifice food's "deliciousness" and pleasurable qualities simply to make cheap calories available to hungry people. We worked hard to put pleasure on the plate, joy in the jabber, but too often joy goes missing in action leaving some ponderous force scowling in your face.

Jim: Slow Food contracted with a women's co-op in Kenya to make posters and bracelets to give us merchandise that promoted joy. We sold some of these items through Slow Food chapters to generate money to send more people of color to Tierra Madre.

But personally, I have to enjoy what I'm doing. If I'm doing social justice work creatively, purposely, effectively, I can't be pissed off. I have friends who are caught up in the negativity, and they often drop out or burn out. You and I are still sitting here holding ground. I guess I learned from my early experience on the picket lines that you can be abused but still come home and be rejuvenated by the common experience of those you were with. And then we'd have a big meal!

We have to overcome the bad experiences—my sister died because of Jim Crow. The hospital had a "colored" waiting room and a white waiting room. She had pneumonia and the hospital made her wait too long. My mother lived that trauma, but there was still a higher calling; we have to keep moving forward and not give in to bitterness.

Mark: You can't be constantly angry and also effective. If you let that moment of violence and rage seize your life, you'll lose sight of the big picture.

Jim: I'm interested in the longer sweep of human existence. We humans have been around for about 2 million years. As a species, we are among the newest. We're still evolving; it's Mandela's "Long March to Freedom," for instance. I always remember that plants and seeds came way before us. I think of myself as stardust condensed into human form, like the particles swirling about in space cohering into heavenly bodies over billions of years.

Mark: We don't honor our history or respect the process of adaptation. I think of the few seconds on the universe's clock that we humans have occupied terra firma. It's truly humbling. But to then look at the incremental progress that has been made to reduce injustice—even when we can sometimes acknowledge great progress—well, it sure tests your resolve.

Jim: Stolen land and stolen labor are the story of food and agriculture. This was the foundational injustice. That Slow Food will acknowledge and adopt this principle soon is a pivotal point for transformation to justice, and clearly a big moment of progress.

The exploitation of the environment mirrors the exploitation of people. The rise of the state was accompanied by the rise of the patriarchy which led to the oppression of women—the Divine, as it has been conceived in most mythology and religion, used to be both male and female, then it became entirely male which brought about assault on nature, including women. The disregard of mother earth became a disregard for women. The good news is that as a species we are maturing because of this realization, and we get to feel alive because we feel a sense of joy.

Mark: If we didn't feel alive, if we don't find joy, we'd be teetering toward mass depression and suicide.

Jim: I loved reading Nietzsche, Lao-tse, Plato, Mumford, and Huxley. They give me a sense of different people's view of humanity and the contradictions. At the very least, I learned that that we're the not first people to suffer. Some of those Black kings and queens enslaved Black people to build the pyramids. They were sons of bitches!

Mark: Intellectually, you have a big project, especially when it comes to helping someone feel that they are not the first person to ever be a victim of another person's exploitation and greed.

Jim: Marx's analysis of capitalism is that the person who spends their life assembling widgets day after day is only given a diminished view of their history and humanity. A person with a larger sense of themselves won't work for the man. Helping people get to that point is my ultimate objective.

Mark: My first encounter with you was maybe twenty years ago in Lexington, Kentucky, at a local food summit. There were 150 people in the room, 99 percent of whom were white, and you were leading the discussion. I thought that was interesting. Everybody was totally engaged because of your aura and facilitation skills. Though you seem continuously buoyed by faith, I've always been curious about the larger source of that aura.

Jim: Again, I had three great-grandfathers who fought in the Civil War, and they were fighting for their own freedom as well as that of their wives and children. My family has always been engaged, even when they were enslaved, even when they were property. My mother was confronted with sexual attacks. How did my family know to build schools and churches after Emancipation? They knew they only had one direction to go, and that was up.

Mark: Yet, in your professional life, you must have had your share of dark moments and push back?

Jim: Some of my family called me and told me to be careful about this journey. One of my cousins said they would pray for me. If you're an activist, you're a marked person. I've been stopped by the police; I've had police point guns at me; I've had the FBI come to my house. As an African-American, that happens all the time.

Mark: Your response, as well as that of other members of the Black community, almost seems Christ-like—everyday you're crucified; you could stay in a tomb of hostility, resentment, and anger, or, like Christ, you roll back that stone and get on with the work.

Jim: Somedays on a farm, a flood comes along and wipes out your field; or the coyotes take out your chickens; you can't give up or dwell on the past. You need to heal or you'll do things that make things worse. I was taught a faith in myself; you can weather this storm if you can look back and laugh at what happened.

Mark: I got one more question for you, but I want to make sure you're okay. We've been talking now for almost three hours. It looks like we're the last people in the restaurant. Do you need a break, or a walk around the block?

Jim: I could do this all day! In my view, what's missing in the movement is an opportunity to have just these kinds of conversations.

Mark: So, my question is this: We are two guys who devoted their lives to community work. But unlike past presidents, we're unlikely to be spending our later years planning our national libraries. What's our role, what's our work at this stage in our lives?

Jim. As elders, we have experienced seven decades of life. Our work is to synthesize our past and the past work of others, and then to share that synthesis. To help future generations develop a more integrated view, one that will allow them to look forward and backwards at the same time. We need to have a vision based on a synthesis of past, present, and future, like the West African bird whose head is facing to the rear to know where he's come from. Like I said, to exploit people, the plantation and factory owners needed to give them a diminished view of the past. They accomplished those ends with stolen land, stolen people, and enforced their work with violence. As H. Rap Brown said, "Violence is as American as cherry pie."

Mark: How appropriate for today! That could be the NRA's motto.

Jim: Yes, the Second Amendment is used as a way for capital and power to control others through guns and violence.

But what's our work? Synthesis. I was blessed in my life to be in the presence of elders who themselves synthesized for me and others. Generational disconnect is real. Part of our work as elders is to reach out to younger generations. Whenever I can, I sit around over breakfast and have conversations; sit around over dinner and have conversations. My mantra is to bring light in and send light out. Real simple. That's the work.

Humans are social beings but are suffering from a form of psychic hunger. Much of our episodic violence is a result of their isolation, of people wanting a sense of relationship but not getting it. There is a psychic hunger that results from dead Kentucky coal towns with their boarded-up buildings and the remaining people on opioids. If people don't have access to creative outlets—if they can't see beyond a set of diminished possibilities—that psychic hunger will lead to destructive behavior.

I'm some time referred to as that crazy-ass farmer from Kentucky, but our work is synthesizing, and to connect with young folks.

Mark: And to bring joy, which you have done for me tonight! Thank you.

CHAPTER THIRTEEN

New Jersey = Tomato

October, 2023

Food system change is often associated with non-profit organizations, small farmers, and public policy advocates. But if deep and lasting change is to occur—change that is normalized and even institutionalized within the structures of food production, distribution, and consumption—then successful for-profit businesses are a necessity as long as we continue to operate within some kind of capitalist, market-driven economic system. Much attention has been directed, rightfully so, to farmers who are the foundation of a new, just, and sustainable order, but much less light has been shed on the role of processors and others involved in the food distribution chain. Like farming—and like effective non-profit and advocacy organizations—vision, leadership, imagination, and entrepreneurship are vital to the success of other food system enterprises. The essay that follows looks at how those elements are applied in a small food processing business. Biggest surprise: Canned marinara sauce can be really good!

Yes, I'm from New Jersey. After years of therapy, I now proudly and openly embrace the place of my birth and coming of age, both for its physical attributes as well as its hard-earned state of mind. With that acceptance, of course, comes an acknowledgment of its contradictions. The much-coveted Jersey Shore and lush Pine Barrens stand in stark contrast to the refineries of Bayonne and the state's contorted roadways, site of many of America's most legendary traffic jams. Celebrities like Sinatra, Springsteen, and Streep inspire and move us, while Jersey's corrupt politicians such as former US Senator Harrison Williams and Camden Mayor Angelo Errichetti (the inspiration for the movie *American Hustle*) repel us. Perhaps it's because of this history and its inconsistencies that I feel a bit nonchalant about the recent indictment of NJ's US Senator Bob Menendez on bribery charges. After all, why shouldn't a guy be allowed to walk around with a little gold bullion in his pockets? You never know when you might need to buy a pack of gum or feed a parking meter.

Aside from its dubious distinction of maintaining a high occupancy rate in the "Jersey Wing" of the Federal Penitentiary, the Garden State's most significant contribution to the world just might be the tomato. As a boy, it's the first vegetable (I know it's a fruit!) I fell in love with after seeing plump red clusters swaying seductively on the vines of my neighbor's backyard garden. Due to its unique configuration of humidity, temperature, and soils, New Jersey, which is essentially a peninsula, produces some of the most flavorful tomatoes in the nation. And, over several decades, the rise in the state's tomato reputation has been aided by the tender and knowing hands of Rutgers University (the State University of New Jersey) plant scientists.

I can hear your groans after reading such a smug assertion. California, Florida, Ohio—you can strut your stuff and make all the noise you want, but I'm prepared to defend my claim to the superiority of my home state's tomatoes with a duel, a means of settling disputes which I believe is still legal in New Jersey. With a bushel full of just-picked, peak of harvest Jersey tomatoes by my side, I'll challenge all comers to meet me at the toll booths off exit 9A on the New Jersey Turnpike. We'll each grab one of our respective tomatoes, and standing back-to-back, take ten strides in the opposite direction, turn, and heave it at the other. Yours may strike me directly in the chest; though knocking me back a foot or two, it will bounce off and skid harmlessly down the pavement like a tennis ball. Mine, however, should it land as intended on your forehead, will splatter luxuriously across your face leaving rich, red trails down your cheeks, flowing into your gaping and eager mouth. Your eyes will open wide, a smile will grace your lips, and New Jersey tomato nirvana will descend upon you.

The Tomato

As good as the many varieties of tomatoes grown in New Jersey are, they face the same limitation as any other fruit or vegetable grown in a temperate zone—seasonality. Whether I'm nursing them along in my New Mexico garden, or a large commercial farmer is producing them for fresh market, you'll be lucky to get eight weeks of respectable, locally grown fresh tomatoes a year, even with the benefit of season extenders (don't talk to me about greenhouse tomatoes or winter tomatoes shipped thousands of miles—they are only useful for batting practice). My personal "season extender" is canning, which when it comes to tomatoes is easy to do in just about any home kitchen. All you need is a large pot for boiling water and a few glass canning jars with lids and tops. I'll produce enough surplus tomatoes from my garden, sometimes supplemented with five to ten pounds of "seconds" from the farmers' market to meet my processed tomato needs for a year.

That's good for my basic cooking needs, but what about that essential tomato sauce for pizza, a menu item so ubiquitous that it seems to be available in every eatery I go to these days (as they say in New Jersey, pizza's not just for pizzerias anymore!). Or what about your favorite "date night" Italian restaurant whose marinara sauce is so good you'd hurl yourself through rings of fire for a mere tablespoon. And how about those poor souls whose craving for ketchup is so powerful that french fries and hot dogs are no more than an expedient form of transportation. Without commercially available processed tomato products, these essential food and menu items would disappear, plunging our reason for living into doubt.

But what if you could have that Jersey tomato terroir all year around, grown by local producers, processed by a small, family-owned business, with taste and quality second to none, distributed at scale to retailers and restaurants within a few hundred-mile radius, and available online to the rest of us who don't have the privilege of living in or near New Jersey? Well, the good news is that you can, and it goes by the company name of First Field (First Field, n.d.). The inspiration and passion for this food business comes from the decidedly non-corporate couple, Theresa Viggiano and Patrick Leger. Together, they spawned a mom-and-pop start-up which transitioned into a fast-growing food processing business that stakes its reputation on the authenticity of "Jersey Grown" and their working relationship with growers and buyers.

First Field

Like many young farmers and food entrepreneurs today, Patrick and Theresa don't have deep agricultural roots. Theresa is a "Jersey Girl" who was doing graduate work at Rutgers on aging and mental illness but always had a passion for gardening. Patrick grew up in North Carolina, earned an MBA at Vanderbilt, but was born in Quebec, which, interestingly, gave the couple their only food processing cred. "We eat more ketchup in Canada per capita than anywhere in the world. We put it on everything," he tells me. So, armed with his mother's homemade ketchup recipe and a bumper crop of tomatoes at their Jersey homestead in the summer of 2013, they made their first batch of ketchup.

You might say the rest is history. Like a garage band that got its first gig at the local VFW hall and then moved on to play stadiums, the couple started selling their backyard tomatoes and ketchup off a card table at the foot of their driveway, with a cigar box for honor payments. Today, First Field's crushed tomatoes, marinara sauce, ketchup, cranberry sauce, and pumpkin puree have elbowed their way onto the shelves of some of the region's most prestigious retailers like Whole Foods and Trader Joe's. Their sauces are gracing the pies of some of the best pizza restaurants in New York City, including the Andrew Bellucci (a.k.a. "The Don of Dough") Pizzeria in Queens. "They like our sauce because it's rich. Pizza dough doesn't like watery sauce!" says Patrick. And their success to date has meant that some of the country's biggest food retailers and service companies are knocking at their door.

In spite of its modest success—annual sales are growing rapidly—First Field is not a rag to riches story, nor does it evoke the purest sentiments of the local food movement. Again, like family farms where at least one member of the household works a non-farm job, Patrick works as a full-time investment advisor, the income from which supports the family (they have two children, ages eight and eleven). Theresa directs the business on a very full-time basis while Patrick fills in with finance and operational work in the evenings and on weekends. Though they have been in business now for a few years, neither one of them takes a salary. This reflects their desire to effectively self-finance the start-up with money from family, friends, and even Equal Exchange, the worker co-op and fair-trade organization that has been expanding its line of domestic products. Patrick and Theresa did take one major step forward in the direction of self-care this summer: they took their first two-week vacation since the business began.

The keeping it close to hearth and home approach is as much a rejection of the usual start-up finance model that relies on venture capitalists, or even a bank with more progressive lending practices, as it is a fervent desire to keep their lives family-focused and ultimately sane. An unstated company policy is that family comes first. That's why the first thing you see when you walk into Food First's modest facility, located in a non-descript commercial business park in central Jersey, is a large day care space that also served as a kind of one-room schoolhouse during the COVID-19 lockdown. To the same end, Patrick and Theresa would probably acknowledge that their most important off the books' "assets" are Theresa's Jersey Shore parents, who provide exceptional grandparenting services.

But one's family values can still be put to the test. On the Sunday afternoon I visited their facility, Theresa was stirring a giant kettle of cranberry sauce to meet a holiday order from a customer ("Thanksgiving comes earlier every year," she said with a sigh) while Patrick was stacking cases of pumpkin puree on a palette for shipment to a pie baker in Boston. Besides the two of them, they have three other full-time employees with a fourth expected to start that Monday. In all likelihood, Theresa's grandparents were supervising the construction of sandcastles on one of the Shore's waning summer days. When the harvests start cascading off the farms, and the customers say they want what they want now, you don't pack your sunscreen and head for the beach.

Getting ahead while keeping your head may be one of the most challenging facets of any business. But staying true to your mission, i.e., a set of values that drive your business, while managing the food system's many headwinds is both an art and a science. Like other idealistic foodies, Patrick and Theresa set off with the hope of controlling every aspect of their supply chain and staying within a well-defined organic lane. They received assistance from the Rutgers University Innovation Center to learn the food processing trade and then piloted their product development at Elijah's Promise, a non-profit job training and community soup kitchen in New Brunswick, NJ. Elijah's Promise gave them a chance to use a commercial kitchen after hours ("we were the 'night shift,'" joked Theresa) to hone their production skills and earn their FDA approval.

Again, with guidance from Rutgers Cooperative Extension, they headed out into the field to find local farm product suppliers. This is where their ideals and early assumptions started to bump up against reality. Hoping to buttress their brand with a strong organic identity, they soon realized that New Jersey's organic growers didn't have sufficient production to meet First Field's demand. Similarly, the growers were small and often producing different tomato varieties. When you're canning commercially, you can't mix 'n' match nor throw whatever's coming off the field into your #10 can. Product performance and consistency are sacrosanct for chefs.

When they talked to conventional tomato growers who were large enough to supply them, "we realized that we were being starry-eyed greenies," said Theresa. In other words, no farmer could get over the high bar they were setting; they were clearly at a crossroads. As Patrick put it, "We had to decide if we wanted to be organic—sure, we could have imported organic tomatoes from Mexico—or did we want to support local." Though New Jersey's twenty-six or so commercial scale tomato growers had consolidated down to six over the past couple of decades, there are thousands of acres of prime New Jersey farmland comprised of well-drained, sandy loam soils producing highly regarded tomatoes for both fresh slicing and canning markets. To the chagrin of the state's organic farming community, First Field chose local commercial scale producers as the most feasible path for their business. According to Patrick, this required them to work harder to build working partnerships with organic farmers over time. This has resulted in First Field's commitment to buying other produce like winter squash, cranberries, and blueberries from small, local farmers to supply the 25 percent of their business that is not tomato based. "Building trust with all our farmers—big and small—is the most important thing we do. We can't just show up one year and not the next. We have to prove we're real year after year after year," said Patrick.

Tomato Land

The New Jersey Turnpike is essentially a northeast region tomato corridor in the middle of one-quarter of the nation's population. The state's farmers are growing vast quantities of tomatoes (some fields are only 100 yards from the turnpike), going to canneries in Pennsylvania, New Jersey, or elsewhere, and then onto the warehouses that serve the wholesale and retail supply chains. In choosing to support local growers and the Jersey identity that goes with it, First Field also chose the one remaining tomato cannery in New Jersey to process and pack their tomatoes. It is owned by a large food conglomerate. According to Patrick, their dream would be to one day have their own cannery and avoid the potentially volatile world of large food corporations. At the moment, their other non-tomato canning takes place at their central Jersey facility.

New Jersey may be a tomato corridor, but it's also the most densely populated state in the country. Land values and development pressure are enormous, but even with New Jersey's Department of Agriculture's courageous efforts to protect farmland, the dike can only hold for so long before the rising waters of sprawling subdivisions bust it loose. As a public policy tool, farmland preservation efforts are really just an interim measure; ensuring that farmland remains working land requires that it's not just protected from the rapacious condo kings, but that it also performs within the parameters set by the food system's marketplace. To that end, First Field is the tip of the market innovation spear. Using the "Jersey Fresh" logo, telling the local Jersey story on their cans and jars, but, perhaps most importantly, proving through the quality and performance of their products that Jersey grown is something more than advertising schmaltz. Rob Everts, a co-director of the fair-trade leader Equal Exchange put it this way: "First Field is an excellent example of a small, socially, and environmentally driven business trying to rebuild the New Jersey tomato industry in a truly sustainable way. We are so inspired by what they are doing that we have invested in their business to try to ensure its success."

The consequences of First Field's success or failure are enormous. Without robust regional connections between farmer, processor, buyer, and eater—ones that are geographically close, not based on cross-country or global shipping—Jersey growers may not be around in ten years. As Patrick put it, "That would be like paving over Napa Valley. It would be an incredible shame!"

The Seed

Cut into a ripe, red tomato, and let the pulp and juice pool up on your cutting board. Carefully separate out some seeds with the tip of a knife and push them to the edge for a few minutes to dry. Select just one by pressing a fingertip gently to it so that it sticks to your skin. Examine it closely and measure it. With my crude measuring instrument, I determined that a single oblong seed from one of my homegrown tomatoes was 3/32nd of an inch wide and 1/8th of an inch long. Inside that tiny hard body doesn't necessarily rest the secrets to the universe, but it's pretty darn close. From my 2023 Johnny's Selected Seeds catalog, I could choose from 103 separate tomato seed varieties, the description for each one touting their unique attributes related to size, shape, color, taste, slicing, saucing, selling, and much more, none of which you'll detect by simply looking at the seed. The one attribute that most varieties shared, including the one stuck to my fingertip that would blow away if I exhaled too hard, is their capacity to produce a large green plant that could, if tended correctly, set five to ten pounds of edible tomatoes. In spite of a passing understanding of the science behind all of this, I still regard that itsy-bitsy thing resting on my pinky as a miracle for its ability to produce large quantities of tomatoes as well as a vast number of characteristics, depending on the variety.

NEW JERSEY = TOMATO

At Rutgers University, miracle and science have found a happy partnership. The original Rutgers tomato, which Wal-Mart refers to as the "Legendary Jersey Tomato," may have indeed been handed down to humankind by the Creator, but its infinite refinements and applications for multiple purposes and settings is decidedly secular. And for large tomato growers who are spending upward of $20,000 a year on seed, getting the right variety for the right purpose at the right time is crucial.

First Field has a similar interest. If the tomato their canner turns into sauce only succeeds in creating a runny pool atop a beautifully hand-thrown pizza crust, a string of Italian, Spanish, or Haitian-Creole accented expletives will fill the restaurant's kitchen, and First Field's phone number will disappear among the salami rinds. That is why they are working closely with Rutgers Professor Tom Orton whose name is spoken with hushed reverence by Patrick. Professor Orton, responsible for the "Rutgers 250" that was written up in *The New York Times*, is now collaborating with First Field to create the perfect sauce tomato that, in turn, will be perfectly suited for South Jersey growing conditions.

Patrick breaks it down for me this way: "A tomato that is too watery will take longer to cook down which uses more energy and robs the tomato of its flavor. We are working with growers to set aside small plots of their land for seed trials. That's one way we're collaborating with our producers." Keep in mind that none of this "seed work" uses genetic engineering (no one's crossing a San Manzano canning tomato with a bunny rabbit). Finding the right processing tomato is a glacial process requiring years of diligent lab and field work, but it is no small part of saving Jersey farmers, farmland, and a big chunk of the northeast food system.

To make the point clear, Patrick brings out a 3-feet by 4-feet wood frame with one side covered in a fine wire mesh screen. Three separate groups of about 200 seeds each lie on the screen. He explains to me how each group contains certain desirable traits that the wizard Professor Orton will combine to bring to fruition, that will in turn be selected for their desirable traits, and so on. I think back on that one, minute specimen perched on my fingertip. Like Henry David Thoreau, I have "a faith in the seed" that, if this whole process is handled correctly, New Jersey might play a big part in saving us from a global food system controlled by a few giant corporations.

The Taste of Liberation

Patrick is fumbling around their makeshift office kitchen for a spoon so that I can sample their sauce. With a little grunting, he opens up a #10 can of crushed tomatoes with one of those little manual butterfly can openers that your grandmother used. I scoop up a spoonful, then another, and swirl it around my palate. This may be the first time in my life I've eaten tomato sauce straight out of a can, but soon I'm contemplating it the way I might a good Bordeau. Do I sense something rich, earthy, even chunky, though the sauce is smooth as silk? Calling upon my limited wine tasting vocabulary, I wonder if I'm savoring notes of New Jersey in this robust red pulp. I realize, in fact, that the joy prancing across my tongue isn't just from the flavor bequeathed to the tomato by my home state's soils, clammy summers, and the rigorous seed massaging of plant scientists. It's a taste of liberation from a dominant food system that only wants to treat you like a comatose consumer and raw food products like they are no more than commodities. First Field is what the alternative tastes like.

CHAPTER FOURTEEN

"I'm Tired of Watching Our Town Die"

October, 2020

The challenges facing rural America are legion. The hollowing out of small towns, declining population, exiting young people, limited job opportunities, and long distances to all kinds of services have defied many social and economic interventions designed to reinvigorate these declining places. As important as programs, investments, and public policy are to finding solutions, the roles that individual entrepreneurs and a motivated citizenry play may be the best determinants of success. From northwestern Kansas, the story of one person's campaign to bring some economic life back to her town stands out for its determination and skill. Biggest surprise: The Elephant Restaurant.

Part One: The First Visit

The vines from the elementary school's sizeable pumpkin patch were sprawling aggressively across the basketball court. In spite of the 98-degree heat, the plants were so vigorous, so verdant, that one could imagine them ascending and eventually encircling the nearby five-story feed mill that dominated Atwood's downtown center. Was this a symbolic challenge from an upstart school garden project—a David and Goliath confrontation, as it were—to the commodity feed and livestock farming that defines western Kansas? Perhaps. But more than likely it's a murmur rising inexorably to a scream from the school's young people that the status quo may not be enough to keep them around. Because if you climbed to the top of that mill, spread before you would be too many vacant store fronts, too little pedestrian or car traffic, and too little future.

What you'd also see from that precarious perch is the rest of Rawlins County, of which Atwood is its largest town. Stretching out against an endless horizon is a vast expanse of wheat and feed crop-covered prairie. No less impressive by its absence, you will not see a single stoplight or much in the way of human habitation. Rawlins County, set firmly against the Nebraska border to the north and one county over from Colorado to the west, makes abundant room for a population of barely 2,500 people (down from 3,400 in 1990), which is hardly a regional anomaly. The entire nine-county northwest Kansas area has a population of only 30,000 inhabiting a territory larger than my former home state of Connecticut, which contains 3.2 million people within its borders.

Against a backdrop of commodity crop dominance and a dwindling population, it's not uncommon to hear some version of a "goodbye to rural America" tune rising from various quarters. But down on Atwood's quiet streets, a different, more uplifting song can be heard from a growing chorus of people working to create a more hopeful future for this beleaguered corner of America. One of those voices is JoEllyn Argabright, who, in one bold act of derring-do early in the summer of 2020 bought out a closing garden store and two adjoining buildings. Her intent is to transform them into a multi-purpose garden center and food hub. When I asked her why, her response was simple: "I'm tired of watching our town die."

When Jo, who is thirty-five, first picked me up for a tour, she identified herself in advance as "the only 5-foot, 3-inch woman in the parking lot with a big black pick-up truck." If there's one thing I've learned from living in the West, don't expect small women to always drive a Prius. In this part of the world, the vehicle is still a projection of your personality. In Jo's case, she's a self-identified "farm wife, mother of two children (two and four years old), Extension educator for Kansas State University, and now a store owner."

Growing up in Boulder as the only child (her one sibling died in childhood) of a single father—a recently retired Denver emergency room physician—she first attended Colorado State University on a clay pigeon shooting scholarship. (This last item—a women's Olympic competition since 2000—took me a while to process since I've seen shotguns longer than Jo is tall.) Transferring after her freshman year to Kansas State, Jo would acquire undergraduate and graduate degrees that led her to a variety of nutrition and community development positions within the University's Extension system. Just as importantly, she met her future husband, Austin, at K-State, after which they would return to his family's farm in Rawlins County.

"My passion is around local food as a way to feed our community," Jo said as she showed me around her newly acquired properties. While that passion partially explains her motivation to open a food hub in a community where new business start-ups are nearly as rare as dodo birds, she appears to be mining a deeper vein of personal desire. "I want to create something my kids will be proud of and that will give them a reason to stay here."

But she also shares a personal drive that has ignited her inner entrepreneur. "As a [Kansas State] Extension educator I'm always helping others with business and farm problems. But I'm preaching to them from the safe space of a university. I need to actually do it myself because, like farming, not enough young people want to become merchants." According to the people I interviewed for this article, Jo is now one of the youngest business owners in the nine-county region.

To say Jo "walks it like she talks it" is an understatement. By her own admission, the comfortable salary she earns from a major state institution places her in the higher echelon of the county's income earners. But rather than seek safe rates of return in the stock market, she's invested her savings, uncompensated time, and Extension knowledge back in the community. Though the purchase price of the store, its inventory, the greenhouse, a vacant lot, and two adjoining buildings—all tightly packed onto about a quarter acre of land—was at bargain basement rates, a significant sum was still required. She dug into her own savings, secured an "investment" from her father ("I had to agree to let him volunteer at the store in return for his gift," she noted with a laugh), and took out a long-term, low-interest loan from Network Kansas, a state-sponsored entrepreneur development fund.

All of that just gave her title to the properties and a chance to make a go of it in a risky marketplace. The "Dream," the thing that gets Jo up in the morning will take more money, massive amounts of community support, and, to use her favorite phrase, "a lot of love." The Dream includes a food hub that features locally produced food and other horticultural products. Already, an heirloom garlic grower wants to sell through the hub, and local beef and pork operations have expressed interest in selling finished retail products there.

A seed-starting greenhouse (Jo has set a goal for the store to start 75 percent of the plants it sells) will be added onto the existing 20 × 48 feet greenhouse. This phase of plan got a boost recently from a $45,000 SPARK grant from the Kansas Department of Commerce as part of the coronavirus stimulus package (Kansas received $9 million in federal funds for local food system promotion). This will include the addition of a walk-in produce cooler and freezer.

Rounding out the entire food center will be a commercial kitchen incubator that will house the equipment, safety training, and other support services necessary to producing and marketing processed food products. Through her Extension work, Jo already has several clients for whom such a facility could launch their much hoped for food businesses. To ignite a food-chain effect, gardening education programs will encourage and support home-scale food production and processing that have surged since the appearance of COVID-19. The store's 2021 calendar of events already has courses on the docket titled "Growing Herbs," "Cooking with Herbs," and "Seeds to Sauce." A café is another logical and likely addition that Jo sees emerging down the road.

Besides this immediate infusion of "emergency" government cash and self-financing, Jo's hybrid non-profit and for-profit corporate model will enable her to tap into other government and private foundation sources. But the biggest and perhaps least visible part of Jo's financing plan will be "goodwill"—that squishy financial concept that businesses often use to beef up their anemic balance sheets. Customers are already buying "gift cards" for spring purchases to augment the store's cash flow, and as many as thirty-five product vendors are extending credit against the coming year's inventory. Chatting with Jo in front of her store late one morning was a lesson in the underlying value of small-town life. A steady trickle of walkers, well-wishers, and honking pick-up truck drivers waved and offered Jo encouragement. In response to a recent request, the local public works director stopped by to trim a beautiful shade tree gracing the store's curbside—a municipal action that normally takes months in places I've lived. Volunteers are already showing up to clean her buildings; high school job-readiness programs will provide apprentice workers; and one citizen has offered to front Jo the funds to support this much-needed business (Jo said, "She told me, 'You can pay me back whenever'"). Call it an old-fashion barn-raising event writ large, a form of community-supported capitalism supplanting the failures of conventional capitalism, or a welling up of social capital that small towns draw on to keep their faltering hearts beating; the goodwill I saw in Atwood is something you can take to the bank.

Jo's store is the train leaving the station that everyone is clamoring to be onboard. As one local resident told me, "We're all longin' for belongin'" meaning that in an area where people often feel socially isolated because they may live miles from the nearest person, the need for "connectedness" becomes palpable. "There's a strange juxtaposition between feeling isolated in a rural community at the same time you feel connected," reflected Jo over lunch at the Mojo Café where we sat with Travis Rickford and Courtney Schamberger. Travis, who is the Executive Director of the Live Well Northwest Kansas, an agency that advocates for the expansion of mental health services, explained that "connection comes when there's a crisis like the way people do when someone dies." But he notes that social isolation is why rural suicide rates are higher than average, and that "togetherness" is not always the answer. "With COVID forcing households to stay closer than normal, we've seen a 200 percent increase in the number of calls to our domestic violence hotline." Travis points out that right now the region has a "perfect storm of things that prevent families from thriving and are contributing to anxiety and depression" including the stressed farm economy (e.g., fluctuating crop prices), COVID, substance abuse (opioid use is high), and the continuing lack of an adequate health-care infrastructure.

These are the burdens that rural America has been carrying for far too long, and ring like sirens in the ears of those under forty years of age. When Jo's youngest child was only one, he stopped breathing in his crib. She revived him but his care required immediate medical helicopter transport to Denver. When the team of specialized pediatric health providers prepared instructions for Jo to pass onto her pediatrician, she nearly choked, "What good is that? I'd have to drive three hours to get to a pediatrician!"

Events like this don't deter a generation of twenty and thirty somethings. If anything, they seem to strengthen their resolve to become the next generation of leaders their communities need. Courtney, who's in her mid-twenties and a vocational agriculture teacher at the local high school, says, "My age group should be stepping up to provide leadership because we are the future of this town. I've only been here four years and I'm already on five boards." She's a little frustrated that more of her peers aren't doing the same, but has faith that her community is going to turn around. "There are more people shopping locally, and mutual support for our businesses, artists, and craftspeople is growing."

Evidence of a trending upward in young people is supported by an enrollment uptick in the number of Rawlins County middle and high school students this year. Overall, a more robust participation by a younger demographic is confirmed by Misty Jimerson, the Coordinator of the nine-county Western Prairie Food Farm and Community Alliance which monitors and supports new food system activity. "We are seeing young folks moving back and starting businesses, including restaurants, that use more locally grown food. This is developing new markets in our region for food that people actually eat."

Another trend gaining traction—one that could not have been predicted—is an influx of coronavirus "refugees" from places like metro-Denver. Like those who left New York City after 9/11, the fear that densely populated urban/suburban areas are more life-threatening is driving people into the arms of low-density, rural areas that may be as much as three- to four-hour drives from "hotspots." According to local real estate agents, the last twelve homes in Hitchcock County, Nebraska (pop. 2,900)—bordering Rawlins County to the north—went to Colorado buyers, as did most of the recent home sales in Herndon, Kansas (pop. 129) located in

Rawlins County. Apparently, these agents have long waiting-lists of out-of-staters searching for rural properties.

Shortly after Jo took possession of her new enterprise, she was pawing through the store's second floor inventory that was not accessible to shoppers. She was startled to find full bottles of DDT and arsenic, substances long banned from agricultural use. The safe removal and disposal of these dangerous vestiges of the region's agricultural past were now Jo's responsibility. In other words, she had inherited the sins of her forbearers, but rather than rail against the injustice, she arranged with the county's hazardous waste disposal facility to take charge of these items. It was a symbolic passing of the torch from an unsustainable form of food production to one that is placing people, community, and the environment at the center of a very local plate. Her discovery reminds us that we don't always like what we find in our parent's attic, but we learn to live with what we can, dispose of that which is intolerable, and set a course for a better future.

In Atwood, Kansas, and across rural America, that course does not include a wholesale rejection of the old, but a reinvention and a Millennial-inspired repurposing of what is already there. "I'm going to run a different kind of business," Jo firmly asserted, "one that is hyper-local with its merchandise, community-oriented in its approach, and based on the proposition that we will thrive, not just survive." As we toured the still disheveled second floor, now purged of its toxic substances and beginning to be reimagined as a healthy, creative space, Jo said, "We just gotta give it some love!" As she knew, that also meant more young people, local food driving a local economy, public and private financing, and a community that believes in itself.

Part Two: One Year Later

Shaking off a case of pandemic cabin fever, I packed my Subaru and set out in early August to see friends and family back East. Along the way, I decided to check in with places I had visited the prior year, including northwest Kansas. Crossing into Kansas from Colorado on Interstate 70, you know where you are without the help of the "Welcome to Kansas" sign. At least a zillion acres of corn dominate the landscape while a noticeable chemical smell (insecticides?) rises from the fields forcing me to roll up my car windows. One roadside billboard that reads "Phosphate ... Done Better!" does little to reassure me.

My first stop was Rexford where I was scheduled to stay at the historic Philip Houston House B&B (originally built by a Sam Houston descendant). The following morning, I found myself being the only customer at the Whistle-Stop, Rexford's only eatery. The gracious lady who cooked for and served me also required me to pray before I ate. As I gazed at plates set before me containing enough caloric firepower to fuel a farmer for a fortnight, I folded my hands, lowered my head, and said to myself, "Please God, don't let this meal kill me."

But as I learned from the past, never give up on Kansas. In what can only be described as a whiplash culinary U-turn, I had dinner with JoEllyn Argabright at The Elephant Restaurant (The Elephant, n.d.) in nearby Hoxie. "Jo," as readers may recall, is the Kansas State Cooperative Extension Specialist who is also the dynamo developer of the Grass Roots Garden Hub (Grass Roots Garden Hub & Floral, Inc., n.d.) in Atwood. According to her, The Elephant is the "go-to" eatery for any special occasion within a 200-mile radius, not only because the atmosphere, service, and food are off the charts, but because there is nothing else comparable for 200-miles. Imagine living in New York and having to drive to Boston for a good meal; not only would you experience FDT (Foodie Delirium Tremors), you would demand federal funding for the development of community culinary infrastructure.

Admittedly, any stranger who would suddenly find themselves driving through Hoxie would soon be looking for the nearest exit. They would never imagine that halfway down Main Street awaits the creation of founder and executive chef Emily Campbell, a young woman who returned to this, her hometown, a few years ago. What awaits, just to give a sample, is an awesome Signature Old Fashion, a feathery 'Ville Raspberry Black Bean Dip, and a succulent, locally sourced bison steak, all intelligently served by a freshly pressed and bow-tied wait-staff. If you ever find yourself crossing Kansas on I-70 west of Salina, exceed posted speed limits, ignore stop lights and signs, and recklessly pass large livestock trucks to get to The Elephant. It's amazing how one wonderful eatery can light up a town.

But it is not only in pleasing the palate that northwest Kansas has redeemed itself. The next day, Jo gives me a tour of the formerly down-and-out garden store she purchased barely one year ago in Atwood. Since her formal opening on May 1st, the Grass Roots Garden Hub's sales are already twice that of the former store's previous annual sales—in less than four months—and is already breaking even. With just the right amount of understatement, Jo says, "I'm learning that I don't suck at business." Indeed, with a new and attractive wooden fence and pergola to shelter plants, new landscaping, and a cleaned outside wall soon to become a major cool sign, the property has dramatically improved since my last visit. A small Saturday morning farmers' market that just opened across the street is a welcome addition to downtown. Jo hopes to incorporate it into her larger food hub plan. With a genuine sense that the store is a shared enterprise, she credits the town's people for her initial progress when she says, "I'm celebrating our success with the community."

Jo has a long way to go before her vision for a for-profit and non-profit community food hub is fully realized. Though she has not purchased a single non-organic garden product since she took over, financial considerations required that she sell off the substantial inventory of chemical fertilizers and sprays she inherited from the previous owner. With a community beautification grant from Atwood, she will demolish two falling down structures next to the store and replace them with one, 80 feet by 120 feet building that will house a store room, community kitchen, retail greenhouse, and event and education space. As Jo puts it, "education is a mission builder and will stimulate sales." So far, the destruction side of that equation is paid for; the construction part is still looking for money, a task she hopes to complete by year's end.

Things are looking up in Atwood, but Jo's days are long. She still works full-time for K-State, and her two children, ages three and five, see the store as their second home. Her father, who had been helping out in the store, has had recent health issues that need tending to. But with her long dark hair held back by a wide, red polka-dot headband, she radiates exuberance. She's excited to show me a few paint flourishes on some shelving, a sheet metal sign made for her by the high school welding class, and a new wooden seed rack she loves. And just in case a few naysayers happen to walk through the door, she has a sign next to the cactus stand that reads "No Pricks Allowed!"

CHAPTER FIFTEEN

Two Million Angry Moms and One Sociologist: *Free For All: Fixing School Food in America*

February, 2010

Food issue writers and researchers have had an impact on how the general population as well as academics and practitioners look at and understand different facets of the food system. Only a few, however, have focused on just the right subject at the right time to not only foster wide-spread discourse but to also leverage real change. Dr. Janet Poppendieck's book Free for All: Fixing School Food in America *addresses the obvious injustices in what and how children eat in our public schools, and how the injustices relate to our national income disparities. But just as importantly, her research methodology is immersive and embodies the best practices of C. Wright Mills's* The Sociological Imagination. *Biggest Surprise: What was once thought unachievable is now becoming standard practice.*

Early in *Free for All: Fixing School Food in America* (2010) former Texas Agriculture Secretary Susan Coombs declares that, "it will take 2 million angry moms to change school food." Based on what we now know of the dreary state of our children's cafeteria fare, there must be at least that many mamas, as well as a good number of papas who are ready to storm the lunch counters. Fortunately for them and America's 55 million students who gulp down something resembling a cafeteria meal every school day, they've been joined by Hunter College sociologist Dr. Janet Poppendieck, who gives us the best reasons yet for unconditional school food reform.

We are already indebted to Poppendieck for her earlier works *Knee Deep in Breadlines* and *Sweet Charity* where she employed her sleuthing skills to unravel the historical contradictions and compounding irrationalities associated with feeding our nation's neediest citizens. As she did then, Poppendieck combines her talents as historian and sociologist with those of an institutional psychologist to help us get in touch with our nation's school food neurosis.

Why, for instance, have we developed three different ways to pay the lunch lady—one for the poor students, one for the nearly poor, and one for those who supposedly drive BMWs to school? The logical answer might be because that's fair; the rich kids should pay more and the government should subsidize the cost of feeding lower income children, as it does currently to the tune of $11 billion annually. But as Poppendieck peels back the layers of the school food onion, we find the issue has always been less about compassion for needy children and more about accommodating political and commercial interests. Harry Truman (school lunch is good for national security), Ronald Reagan (ketchup is a vegetable), nutritionists and "nutrition-ism" (its nutrients that count, not the quality and taste of food), and various agricultural lobbies wanting to unload their farm surpluses are just a sampling of what has driven the school food agenda. Somewhere low on the totem pole you'll find concern for the health and well-being of boys and girls.

Like any parent, I love to regale my own children with tales of the good old days. I tell them about my high school cafeteria which had exactly one vending machine in the 1960s: a mechanically operated metal box that dispensed a red or golden, uncut, unpackaged, and unadorned fresh apple for 25 cents. Far from feeling deprived (my children asked me if my school was the same one attended by Abe Lincoln), we were a healthy and reasonably bright group of young people. But, today, vending machines (I once counted 51 in just one Albuquerque, New Mexico high school) are as ubiquitous as dog droppings in the melting snow. What has happened during the intervening decades?

Poppendieck's jargon-free narrative takes us step-by-step through the deals, concessions, and compromises that have bureaucratized the school food process while simultaneously dumbing down the food. Why is so much processed food used to prepare school meals? Because it's cheaper and "cooking from scratch" kitchens have been removed from the schools. Why does it have to be cheaper when we're talking about feeding our children? Because the federal government (or anyone else for that matter) will not provide enough funding to enable schools to buy fresh, whole ingredients. (And by the way, taxpayers are spending billions of dollars to subsidize corn and soybeans, the prime ingredients in processed food.) Why do we have so many junk food items sold "à la carte" in our schools? Well, in addition to using a French culinary phrase to disguise what is otherwise crappy food, schools must sell these items to those with discretionary cash—supposedly the students driving the BMWs—to compensate for the low reimbursements they receive for meals that meet mandated USDA standards. And on it goes.

Perhaps what I found most astonishing, and central to Poppendieck's thesis, is the evolution of the three-tiered payment system. While the free, reduced-price, and full-pay categories are the "wins" secured by anti-hunger advocates over many years of legislative battles, Poppendieck argues that the cure may have been worse than the disease. The high cost of determining student eligibility, the administrative reporting burdens imposed by USDA, and of course, the stigma that falls on poor students exacts a high toll. On this last point, Poppendieck has this to say: "The biggest problem is the stigma that comes from being different, from being marked as poor, from being unable to pay in a culture that places excessive value on being able to pay."

Poppendieck has a solution that is as elegant as it will be hard to achieve—universal free meals for all students K through 12. She acknowledges the cost, an additional $12 billion per year (our present wars, please note, are costing about the same amount *each month*) that would not only feed all students for free, but also improve the quality of the food.

If the arguments for universal school meals—efficiency, equity, no one excluded—sound eerily familiar, then you've probably been paying attention to the arguments for universal health care. If nothing else, it's certainly ironic to consider the consequences of removing each system's respective middlemen: processed food purveyors for school food, and private health insurers for health care. Might we all be healthier as a result?

In a long chapter called "Local Heroes" Poppendieck acknowledges the pioneering work of many innovative school food directors like Ann Cooper, as well as movements to connect schools to local farms and even create school gardens. These and others have made important contributions, she says, but they all need to be "scaled up" by becoming institutionalized (my word choice here would be "naturalized") into the system. This, by the way, is the role of public policy, and it is why everyone who cares about what our children eat should be in touch with their members of Congress. The future of school food will be decided in the 2010 Child Nutrition reauthorization now before Congress.

Free for All is well researched and written. While Poppendieck studies her subject with the thoroughness of a sociologist, fortunately she doesn't sound like one. We are treated to a careful review of the facts that flow through a lively and personal narrative. The reader is kept closely by her side as Poppendieck travels through school cafeterias and pores over government reports. Along the way we observe, touch, and taste what 55 million American children consume each school day. Most importantly, she tells us why it's the way it is, and how, if we could somehow put ourselves in the little shoes of people smaller than us, we would do everything we could to make it better.

Update: Since Free for All *came out in 2010, enormous progress has been made in all facets of federally sponsored school meals. The 2020/21 pandemic certainly turned a spotlight on how many school-age children are dependent on the various publicly supported school meal programs and also catalyzed an enormous amount of innovation in the way meals were made and distributed to children at the local school district level.* Perhaps most significantly, the application of the universal free school meals concept gained traction, state by state, across the country. According to the Hunter College New York City Food Policy Center, the universal free meals program has been enacted by eight state governments, is actively being considered in twenty-eight states and the District of Columbia, and has so far not been considered by the remaining fifteen states.

CHAPTER SIXTEEN

George McGovern: A Man Ahead of His Time

October, 2012

One can never underestimate the role of a champion for your cause. Bringing an issue to the public fore and making it prevalent in the common consciousness can accelerate solutions or simply just open up difficult topics for discussion for the first time—even when the person doing so took an epic drubbing in a presidential election. Cultivating champions—and sometimes just finding them—can be an art form that takes time and persistence, but it's a task that should never be neglected. The champion does not have to be a national figure; he or she can be a local or state official; sometimes a celebrity with modest public recognition. And sometimes, as in this case, they just appear, but that doesn't mean you're not always on the lookout for that name who voluntarily becomes a spokesperson. Biggest surprise: I said exactly the right thing at the right time!

I was standing in the ambassador's reception line nervously chatting with those closest to me. In spite of the wine that I was gulping more than sipping, and the charm of a balmy September evening in Rome, I was growing more anxious as I waited my turn on the terrace at 14 Vicolo Antoniniano. This was the Italian residence of the American Ambassador to the United Nations Food and Agriculture Organization where I and my colleagues from the US delegation to the 2000 Conference on Food Security were about to meet Ambassador George McGovern and his wife.

Though the exotic location populated by important people had over-stimulated my senses, it was more the prospect of what I would say to Ambassador McGovern that was fast undoing me. True, I had never met an ambassador before and the number of high-level politicians whose hands I'd shaken could be counted on one hand. But this wasn't any ambassador or politician; it was George McGovern—the first presidential candidate I had ever voted for, a fervent opponent of my generation's war in Vietnam, and possibly the best-known elected official to work tirelessly to end hunger and malnutrition.

There were only three people ahead of me in line. I had less than five minutes to come up with something brilliant to say, something that would at least rescue me from drowning in my own pool of sycophantic drool. As I lifted my hand to his, it came to me, from my heart I think, which is always the best place if only your brain gets out of the way. I told him that his work as co-chair, with Senator Robert Dole of the Senate Committee on Nutrition had been an inspiring and seminal event for my career and for thousands of other young people who chose community food activism as their path to social change.

Ambassador McGovern seemed to hold his smile and my hand a little longer than those before me. In his easy South Dakota drawl, he earnestly thanked me and went on to say at some length that he had just run into Senator Dole at a recent Washington function. They had both agreed that their service on the nutrition committee was among the most important and meaningful of their careers. He said he was truly touched by my compliment and thanked me for sharing it with him. I thanked him, he thanked me, and I thanked him again. It was time for me to move on.

It's hard to imagine another person whose public persona and actions were such a touchstone for my life. As I marched on Washington to protest the insanity of the Vietnam War and later faced jail time for my refusal to comply with orders of the Selective Service System, George McGovern's voice became my voice; he spoke for me and to me. He was a bed rock of consistency and principle that never let me down, and if this sounds like a homily for today's class of politicians whose positions waft like loose pigeon feathers in the wind, then so be it.

McGovern, however, was also a loser. He had been stomped badly in the 1972 presidential election by Richard Nixon whose Watergate antics had not yet been revealed but would soon leave a permanent hurt on the American political experience. Rather than wage a less principled campaign that might have endeared him to more Americans, presidential candidate McGovern chose to speak out against a nonsensical war that was then long beyond futile. He also spoke out against poverty and hunger, subjects that have never been popular enough to win over a majority of American voters. For speaking the truth, he was rewarded with 38 percent of the popular vote, the electoral votes of Massachusetts and the District of Colombia, and the scarlet letters "LL" for "Liberal Loser."

After taking such a beating, he could have easily retreated forever to the plains of South Dakota, but instead chose to expand his fierce advocacy for ending both domestic and world hunger. By making the association between hunger, poverty, equity, and sound nutrition, he remained ahead of the pack. As a re-elected Senator in 1974, McGovern led the Senate Nutrition Committee into on-going investigations into the link between the rising tide of hunger in the US and domestic poverty. Perhaps most importantly and with prescience we can only appreciate today, the Committee issued its now famous 1977 *Dietary Goals for the United States* that made it clear that the growing prevalence of salt, sugar, and fat in our diet was having grave consequences for the country's health. It called for a change in the way we ate, but, like Vietnam, not enough of the right people paid attention.

I'm sure there will be ample competition for the epitaph on George McGovern's headstone, but somewhere engraved in granite and read aloud until everybody hears it should be these words from the Senate Select Committee on Nutrition:

[Hunger] is not [so much] the mechanics of the food assistance programs as it is the fact of persistent poverty, and the continued tolerance in this country of a starkly inequitable distribution of income. In a nation ... in which 40 million people remain poor [43 million for 2023] or near poor, more than a food stamp or child-feeding program is at issue.

His life was a testament to peace, truth, and the promise that all should eat well.

PART THREE
Actions

CHAPTER SEVENTEEN

When Handouts Keep Coming, the Food Line Never Ends

November 18 (Sunday), 2007

The following piece was first published in the Washington Post *on November 18, 2007. It appeared as the lead article on the front page of the opinion section and was highlighted with an entire half-page (top of the fold) image of Andy Warhol's "Campbell Soup Cans." I knew the piece—essentially a promotion for my upcoming book,* Closing the Food Gap *(Beacon Press, 2008)—was likely to be controversial since it offered a strong critique of the bourgeoning food banking sector. But I made two mistakes: the op-ed was released on the Sunday before Thanksgiving, the height of the annual food donation marathon, and I volunteered my email address at the end of the piece in hopes that a modest dialogue might ensue. Anything but: according to the* Post's *Opinion Page editor, the piece had 86,000 hits on their website in the first three days; I received over 400 emails (two-thirds agreed with me); and 200 calls were registered during a scheduled one-hour call-in session (I only had enough time to respond to ten). Biggest surprise: Though critical of food banking methods, a large number of people within that community agreed with me.*

How can anyone not get caught up in the annual Thanksgiving turkey frenzy? At the food bank I co-founded in Hartford, CT, November always meant cheering the caravans of fowl-laden trucks that roared into our parking lot. They came on the heels of the public appeals for "A bird in every pot," "No family left without a turkey," and our bank's own version—"A turkey and a 20 [dollar bill]."

Like pompom girls leading a high school pep rally, we revved up the community's charitable impulse to a fever pitch with radio interviews, newspaper stories and dramatic television footage to extract the last gobbler from the stingiest citizen. After all, our nation's one great day of social equity was upon us. In skid row soup kitchens and the gated communities of hedge-fund billionaires alike, everyone was entitled, indeed expected, to sit down to a meal of turkey with all the fixings.

And here we are, putting on the same play again this year. But come Friday, as most of us stuff more leftovers into our bulging refrigerators, 35 million Americans will take their place in line again at soup kitchens, food banks, and food stamp offices nationwide. The good souls who staff America's tens of thousands of emergency food sites will renew their pleas to donors fatigued by their burst of holiday philanthropy. Food stamp workers will return to their desks and try to convince mothers that they can feed their families on the $3 per person per day that the government allots them. The cycle of need—always present, rarely sated, never resolved—will continue.

Unless we rethink our devotion to food donation.

America's far-flung network of emergency food programs—from Second Harvest to tens of thousands of neighborhood food pantries—constitutes one of the largest charitable institutions in the nation. Its vast base of volunteers and donors and its ever-expanding distribution infrastructure have made it a powerful force in shaping popular perceptions of domestic hunger and other forms of need. But in the end, one of its most lasting effects has been to sidetrack efforts to eradicate hunger and its root cause, poverty.

As sociologist Janet Poppendieck made clear in her book Sweet Charity, there is something in the food banking culture and its relationship with donors that dampens the desire to empower the poor and take a more muscular, public stand against hunger.

It used to be my job to scour every nook and cranny of Hartford for food resources, and I've known the desperation of workers who saw the lines of the poor grow longer while the food bank's inventory shrank. The cutback in federal support for social welfare programs triggered by the Reagan administration in the 1980s unleashed a wave of charitable innovation and growth not seen since the Great Depression. As demand for food rose unabated—as it does to this day—our food bank's staff became increasingly adept at securing sustenance from previously unimaginable sources.

No food donation was too small, too strange, or too nutritionally unsound to be refused.

I remember the load of nearly rotten potatoes that we "gratefully" accepted at the warehouse loading dock and then promptly shoveled into the dumpster once the donor was safely out of sight. One of our early food bank meetings included a cooking demonstration by a group of local entrepreneurs who were trying to develop a market for horse meat. The product's name was Cheva-lean, taken from *cheval*, the French word for horse. The promoters reminded us that the French, the world's leading authorities on food, ate horse meat, implying that therefore our poor clients could certainly do the same. The only thing that topped that was when we had to secure recipes from the University of Maine to help us use the moose parts proudly presented by representatives of the Connecticut Fish and Game Division who'd been forced to put down the disoriented Bullwinkle found wandering through suburban back yards.

We did our job well, and everything grew: Over twenty-five years, the food bank leapfrogged five times from warehouse to ever-vaster warehouse, finally landing in a state-of-the-art facility that's the equal of most commercial food distribution centers in the country. The volunteers multiplied to 3,000 because the donations of food, much of it unfit for human consumption, required many hands for sorting and discarding. The number of food distribution sites skyrocketed from five in 1982 to 360 today.

But in spite of all the outward signs of progress, more than 275,000 Connecticut residents—slightly less than 8.6 percent of the state's residents—remain hungry or what we call "food insecure." The Department of Agriculture puts 11 percent of the US population in this category.

The overall futility of the effort became evident to me one summer day in 2003 when I observed a food bank truck pull up to a low-income housing project in Hartford. The residents had known when and where the truck would arrive, and they were already lined up at the edge of the parking lot to receive handouts. Staff members and volunteers set up folding tables and proceeded to stack them with produce, boxed cereal, and other food items. People stood quietly in line until it was their turn to receive a bag of pre-selected food.

No one made any attempt to determine whether the recipients actually needed the food, nor to encourage the recipients to seek other forms of assistance, such as food stamps. The food distribution was an unequivocal act of faith based on generally accepted knowledge that this was a known area of need. The recipients seemed reasonably grateful, but the staff members and volunteers seemed even happier, having been fortified by the belief that their act of benevolence was at least mildly appreciated.

As word spread, the lines got longer until finally the truck was empty. The following week, it returned at the same time, and once again the people were waiting. Only this time there were more of them. It may have been that a donor-recipient co-dependency had developed. Both parties were trapped in an ever-expanding web of immediate gratification that offered the recipients no long-term hope of eventually achieving independence and self-reliance. As the food bank's director told me later, "The more you provide, the more demand there is."

My experience of twenty-five years in food banking has led me to conclude that co-dependency within the system is multifaceted and frankly troubling. As a system that depends on donated goods, it must curry favor with the nation's food industry, which often regards food banks as a waste-management tool. As an operation that must sort through billions of pounds of damaged and partially salvageable food, it requires an army of volunteers who themselves are dependent on the carefully nurtured belief that they are "doing good" by "feeding the hungry." And as a charity that lives from one multimillion-dollar capital campaign to the next (most recently, the Hartford food bank raised $4.5 million), it must maintain a ready supply of well-heeled philanthropists and captains of industry to raise the dollars and public awareness necessary to make the next warehouse expansion possible.

Food banks are a dominant institution in this country, and they assert their power at the local and state levels by commanding the attention of people of goodwill who want to address hunger. Their ability to attract volunteers and to raise money approaches that of major hospitals and universities. While none of this is inherently wrong, it does distract the public and policymakers from the task of harnessing the political will needed to end hunger in the United States.

The risk is that the multibillion-dollar system of food banking has become such a pervasive force in the anti-hunger world, and so tied to its donors and its volunteers, that it cannot step back and ask if this is the best way to end hunger, food insecurity and their root cause, poverty.

During my tenure in Hartford, I often wondered what would happen if the collective energy that went into soliciting and distributing food were put into ending hunger and poverty instead. Surely it would have a sizable impact if 3,000 Hartford-area volunteers, led by some of Connecticut's most privileged and respected citizens, showed up one day at the state legislature, demanding enough resources to end hunger and poverty. Multiply those volunteers by three or four—the number of volunteers in the state's other food banks and hundreds of emergency food sites—and you would have enough people to dismantle the Connecticut state capitol brick by brick. Put all the emergency food volunteers and staff and board members from across the country on buses to Washington, to tell Congress to mandate a living wage, health care for all and adequate employment and child-care programs, and you would have a convoy that might stretch from New York City to our nation's capital.

But what we have done instead is to continue down a road that never comes to an end. Like transportation planners who add more lanes to already clogged highways, we add more space to our food banks in the futile hope of relieving the congestion.

We know hunger's cause—poverty. We know its solution—end poverty. Let this Thanksgiving remind us of that task.

Update: Other than the avalanche of feedback that followed the initial release of this piece and the subsequent publication of my book, it's nearly impossible to measure the impact a single piece of public writing has on any particular object or events. But in the case of food banking, two significant changes have occurred over the eighteen years since this piece appeared. The first has been a significant improvement in the nutritional quality, especially more fresh produce, in the food bank receiving and distribution chain; the second has been a much greater emphasis on public policy advocacy by the food banks and their associations. These changes may not be universal, but both trends are now recognized and accepted practices within the higher echelons of food banking. I will claim that timely advocacy on my part as well as others contributed to moving the needle on changes that were necessary to refocus the work of food banks away from charity and toward justice.

CHAPTER EIGHTEEN

Welcome to the Weight Wars

April, 2023

One of the most significant consequences of a declining food system has been the astronomical growth in overweight, obesity, and diabetes, particularly among the US population. Compounding injustices include higher rates for people of color as well as more limited health care options for lower income and uninsured people. Recent changes in national political leadership and possible new policy approaches at the federal level portend changes that may take years before their intended outcomes are proven effective (or not). For instance, semaglutides like Ozempic and Wegovy are medications that may change the entire weight management landscape, without necessarily changing the underlying food system and related socioeconomic influences. In the meantime, understanding the evolution of the problem, its impact on the nation's health, the continuing increase in our knowledge of the causes and treatments, and how human behavior and attitudes relate to policies and practices are essential to eventually curtailing a national health crisis. Biggest surprise: Obesity is a more complicated condition than I thought, even after working on it for thirty years.

Childhood obesity is very much in the news these days, as well as it should be. Reflecting back over several decades of work in the community food field, it feels incomprehensible to me that one in five American children now (compared to one in twenty in 1980) fall into the body mass index (BMI) obesity danger zone. BMI is the most accepted measurement of healthy/unhealthy weight, though by itself it is not an indication of any specific medical condition. In 2013, however, the American Medical Association officially recognized obesity as a chronic disease. Over 220 health conditions have been linked to obesity, not the least of which is that obese children run a high probability of becoming obese adults with greater risk of even more health complications. According to a *New England Journal of Medicine* projection, 57 percent of today's two-year-olds will be obese by the time they reach thirty-five (Ward et al., 2017).

I find so much of this data frightening, perhaps, because my awareness of body size as an issue has surfaced gradually over the course of my lifetime. My first recollection was an incident that occurred when I was eleven years old. As I was leaving my New Jersey elementary school one sunny spring afternoon, I noticed a circle of classmates staring at the ground in front of them. Elbowing my way into the silent crowd, I saw two of my classmates, Davey and Richie, locked in a brutal playground brawl. Davey had pinned Richie to the ground with his knees while his hands were locked in a death grip around his throat. "What's going on?" I asked to no one in particular. "Richie called Davey 'fat-so'" was the reply. I knew that Davey, certainly on the chubby side, was the only kid in the school who'd likely pass for overweight today, and that Richie, always a wise guy, loved picking on him.

At that moment, much to our impotent horror, Richie was paying the price. His eyes were bulging, his face was beet-red, and, except for a few gasps of breath, he was nearly motionless. Fortunately, two male teachers jumped into the fray and pulled Davey off, hauling him away to God knows where while the school nurse administered first-aid to Richie. The rest of us, in a state of shock, were disbursed, replete with enough grist for weeks' worth of boyish gossip.

The fight today, the one that has escalated well beyond a playground tussle, is over our individual and national approach to obesity, weight, diet-related disease, body size, and a host of other terms that increasingly carry fraught associations. What has exacerbated the fight, at least partially, is the lack of consensus among experts as to obesity's cause. At one recent international gathering of researchers in the United Kingdom, a biologist offered this assessment of the days-long debate: "There's no consensus whatsoever about what the cause of it is (Belluz, 2022)." In other words, obesity is a far more complex issue than most of us have thought.

Take the study of genetics, for instance. There is a genetic component to human obesity that accounts for 40 percent to 50 percent of the variability in body weight status, and that is substantially higher in individuals with obesity and severe obesity (about 60 percent to 80 percent). After controlling for BMI, science has learned that the genetic contribution to the accumulation of harmful forms of fat ranges from 30 percent to 55 percent (Bouchard, 2021). In fact, we now know that, "227 genetic variants involved in different biological pathways ... have been associated with polygenic [involvement of multiple genes] obesity" (Pigeyre et al., 2016). In addition to polygenic contributions, there are some known single-gene causes of obesity. For example, genes that regulate hunger, (e.g., in the MC4R pathway) underly the cause of a portion of the approximately 5 million individuals in the US who experience early-onset, severe obesity (Uncovering Rare Obesity, n.d.).

Such advances are bringing us ever closer to the new age of personalized medicine, where we will be able to see how genetic factors affect the outcome and choice of obesity treatments. With more studies being conducted, the introduction of precision obesity treatment is brought nearer. According to one paper, "We can predict that, in the future, when receiving a new patient in our obesity department, we will be able to determine the patient's personal responses to the different treatments through genetic testing, so that we can choose the most appropriate method."

I highlight the role of genetics in some detail to illustrate just one of many complicated sets of contributors to the obesity crisis. As I was doing my community work in Hartford, Connecticut, a city with a high poverty rate, I witnessed the transformation of body sizes take place literally before my eyes. In the 1970s and 1980s, hunger and food insecurity, associated with rising food prices and poverty, were the dominant food threats. By the 1990s, overweight, obesity, and the increase in diet-related illnesses such as diabetes had eclipsed hunger. That made sense as we saw the city morph into a food desert and food swamp as the supermarkets exited and fast-food joints proliferated. Our response then was a multi-faceted strategy to effectively flood lower income neighborhoods with healthy, affordable food, accompanied by nutrition education. I can say in retrospect that our impact was limited because it was too narrow. Certainly, something more comprehensive was called for.

Into the evolving path of our growing understanding has stepped a variety of interesting and competing ideas about how to address the problem, including the possibility that obesity is not really a problem at all. In fact, terms like obese or overweight are being replaced by such descriptors as "large-bodied people," and the belief that people of any size can be healthy, regardless of what their BMI levels suggest. Even the use of BMI as a health indicator has been called into question. One proponent of the concept of healthy at any size goes as far as to distribute cards to parents before their children's doctor exams that say, "Don't Weigh Me!" as a rejection of weight as a health indicator, and to protect children from stigmatization. One dietitian told me that she removed the word "Weight" from the title of a book she authored because she knew the word's use had become too controversial.

Underlying much of the debate is the belief that by diagnosing someone as "obese" or "overweight" and prescribing a weight reduction plan and other interventions under the supervision, for instance, of a registered dietitian, brands the child with a Scarlet "F" (for "Fat"). Even more, any discussion or suggestion that someone or a group of people have weight issues can create, in the minds of some advocates, a "body toxic environment" where "weight-shaming" is one of the chief pollutants.

Health at Every Size (HAES) is one group that associates "weight-centered bias" and "policies discriminating against fat people" with racism and oppression of Black people. One of their principles is to "reject the idealizing or pathologizing of specific weights" and, rather than dieting, recommends "eating for well-being," and rather than physical activity, promotes "life-enhancing movement to the degree that they choose." In other words, the celebration of one's body is placed above any medical or cultural pressure to alter its size.

Returning for a moment to Davey, I don't think I could find a better case study for the harm that stigmatization can cause. Having remained in contact with numerous schoolmates over the years, one hears—allowing for the hyperbole that old men are prone to—how Davey's legend continues. There is agreement that he was expelled from junior high school for throwing a desk at a teacher. Similarly verified is how his childhood weight-shaming and resulting rage were channeled into arguably acceptable uses including stints in the Marine Corps, CIA, and Drug Enforcement Agency.

Looking at the 600-plus beautiful teenage faces in my high school graduation yearbook, I couldn't find more than a handful that had retained even a moderate amount of baby fat. A glance at randomly selected American high school yearbooks today would find 19 percent of the students obese and another 16 percent overweight, numbers that carry predictable population-wide health consequences. Along with gun violence, school lockdowns, anxiety, and mental health issues, including suicide, today's young people face an ever-steeper climb to a healthy and productive adulthood. For the high school graduating class of 1968, the only "public health crisis" we faced, other than perhaps the Vietnam War, was teenage acne, a condition we referred to as our "zit-geist."

While fat-shaming and body stigmatization cause harm, and even more to the point, may make the recipient of such messages unreceptive to any intervention (or worse, susceptible to eating disorders like bulimia), we cannot ignore the looming health crisis apparent in the nation's soaring obesity figures. According to the Centers for Disease Control and Prevention, the US obesity prevalence was 41.9 percent in 2020 compared to 30.5 percent in 2000 (Centers for Disease Control and Prevention, 2021). During the same time, the prevalence of severe obesity increased from 4.7 percent to 9.2 percent (Centers for Disease Control and Prevention, 2021). Obesity-related conditions include heart disease, stroke, type

2 diabetes, and certain types of cancer. These are among the leading causes of preventable, premature death.

The estimated annual medical cost of obesity in the United States was nearly $173 billion in 2019 dollars (Zachary et al., 2021). Medical costs for obese adults were $1,861 higher than for people with healthy weight. The cost to the economy is estimated at $90 billion annually due to lost worker productivity. And since a public health crisis is a terrible thing to waste, opportunistic entrepreneurs have nourished a weight loss and diet management market now valued at over $84 billion in revenues for 2021 (projected to reach $130 billion in 2027). The demand is driven by increasing obesity and diabetic populations, fitness/diet companies' promotional strategies, rise in disposable income, and affordable cost of bariatric surgeries.

As we've come to expect in a racially inequitable America, people of color get less of the good stuff and more of the bad stuff, particularly health problems. Non-Hispanic Black adults had the highest age-adjusted prevalence of obesity (49.9 percent), followed by Hispanic adults (45.6 percent), non-Hispanic white adults (41.4 percent) and non-Hispanic Asian adults (16.1 percent).

Those are the numbers, and as best as we know at this time, those are the facts. So why does it seem as if the lifeboat that should be rescuing our children can't find a course? When I read and listen to child health advocates stress stigma avoidance over even the most modest of dietary and physical activity interventions, I often find myself incredulous, especially after reading the summation of the Academy of Nutrition and Dietetics' statement on the problem of childhood obesity, which I quote here at length:

Childhood obesity adversely affects the endocrine, cardiovascular, orthopedic, gastrointestinal, and pulmonary systems. It's associated with greater risk of CVD [cardiovascular disease] later in life. Two risk factors of CVD more common in obese children than in healthy-weight children are hypertension and elevated cholesterol. In one study, 70 percent of obese children had at least one CVD risk factor, and 39 percent had two or more. Other studies have shown increased risk of impaired glucose tolerance, insulin resistance, and type 2 diabetes. Childhood obesity also is associated with breathing problems, such as sleep apnea and asthma. Moreover, obese children are likely to develop joint problems and musculoskeletal discomfort. They're at greater risk of having fatty liver disease, gallstones, and gastroesophageal reflux (i.e., heartburn). Many of these comorbidities that used to be considered "adult diseases" are now regularly seen in obese children.

If 70 percent of obese children have at least one CVD risk factor, how can we countenance such a low-key, almost passive approach to "large-bodied children" that in all likelihood will consign millions to a lifetime of ill-health and possibly premature death? I certainly loved my "look" in college, a filter-less Pall Mall cigarette dangling from my pouty lips that, with my long hair gave me the rebellious image that my classmates and I strove so hard to cultivate. But when it finally dawned on me that my pack-a-day image enhancers would put me in an early grave, I tossed them in the trash.

Fortunately, there are strategies that, when applied in a systems-like fashion, hold promise of stemming the tide of obesity and overweight. They can be found in a summary version in *Today's Dietitian* (Balkenbush, 2018.). In addition to what can be done at the individual or family level, the options for action include the need to eliminate food deserts, an increase in the availability of affordable, healthy foods like fresh fruits and vegetables, and a vigorous push-back against the food industry which pumps ultra processed foods into our nation's veins. And what's key in all of these approaches is the need for better collaboration between all of the stakeholders.

I'm also happy to see the Biden–Harris administration step up to the challenge with both the *National Strategy on Hunger, Nutrition, and Health* and a proposed federal budget that puts our money where their mouths are. Food insecurity, a poor diet, physical inactivity, and ill-health often walk down the same road. It's heartening to see the federal government making strong recommendations to attack these problems in a more or less joined-up fashion.

As I looked over the evidence of what works and the general attitudes and positions of the different camps, one theme appeared to loosely unite everyone's perspective on child obesity—the role of parents/adults. The first interesting fact that struck me is that the prevalence of obesity is lowest among college graduates (26.3 percent) compared to those holding no more than a high school diploma (35.5 percent). While this does not imply that less educated people will be less healthy role models, it does underscore the need for parents to pay attention to their children's health and even take an assertive position when necessary. *Today's Dietitian* reinforces this notion by placing parents at center stage for developing healthy eating behaviors. They state that the "Prevention of childhood obesity should begin early in life, during the fetal period and the first two years of life. In addition to learned behaviors, long-term taste preferences are developed in utero and during breast-feeding. Children are likely to prefer the foods their mothers exposed them to at these stages."

When we look at the way the Women, Infant, and Children (WIC) program operates, we see the emphasis for nutrition counseling placed on the mother. If mom has dietary issues, working with her to correct problems will hopefully spill over into her children's eating behavior and physical activity patterns. A modest reduction in obesity among 2- to 4-year-olds in the WIC program (from 15.9 percent to 13.9 percent since 2010) gives this emphasis some credence. And with the focus of the Biden–Harris Administration on WIC bringing the number of eligible participants up from 50 percent to 60 percent, the positive health impacts of the program are likely to spread further.

A consistent emphasis on working primarily with parents seems to also be supported by the anti-stigma advocates. Registered Dietitian Jill Castle, director of the popular website and podcast "The Nourished Child," is a strong proponent of a "whole child approach" to weight and health matters. While she strenuously opposes any messages or actions that might make a child feel "unworthy," Castle stresses the need to help parents set up healthy lifestyles which will also influence their children. Like many nutritionists and dietitians who are focused on stigma avoidance, she's not a big fan of doctors who don't seem to use the correct language when discussing children's weight and/or health issues. She says the doctor should talk only with the parent(s) about these matters and "keep the children out of the room!"

As I cast my eyes over what increasingly looks like a battlefield, but one on which everyone wants the same thing—the health and well-being of our children—one poignant memory comes to mind. Some twenty-five years ago, the organization I ran, the Hartford Food System, hosted a job slot for a high school student doing community service work. In this case, the student was a young Black woman who happened to be very overweight. On her third day with us, she brought a liter-size bottle of Coke to work and put it in the office refrigerator. I passed her at a moment when she was taking a break and pouring herself a large glass of Coke. With little or no thought in advance, I said something to the effect that she might want to try water once and a while to quench her thirst. She looked at me funny, proceeded to finish her Coke, and when she left for the day, she never came back. I knew I had blown it, and I regret to this day saying what I said.

We cannot deny the long-term toll that childhood obesity will take on today's young people any more than we can shame others for the size and shape of their bodies. At the very least, we know the latter doesn't work, and for the sake of those who are obviously at risk for a lifetime of health complications, we as parents, health providers, and community activists are irresponsible if we tiptoe around our nation's looming public health crisis. A culture of acceptance and avoidance is no substitute for a sensitive society committed to the health and preservation of their children. To that end, those with the most experience and the most evidence must collaborate on a plan to reduce childhood obesity and promote the healthiest children possible.

CHAPTER NINETEEN

Love in the Time of Corona

March, 2020

There hasn't been anything quite like the COVID-19 pandemic in a long time to test the food system and the way by which communities, government, and other institutions respond to a significant threat. In spite of the many disruptions that occurred in the food chain, the system's overall performance proved resilient, despite the many claims that it was irreparably broken. Local and regional food producers and distributors showed their mettle by maintaining and sometimes expanding their supplies and services. Previously lumbering institutions like USDA and the nation's school systems became limber as they discarded rules and regulations and embraced innovation. And the "we" triumphed over the "I" time and again as people found a very good reason—even if it was only for their survival—to collaborate and put others before themselves. Biggest surprise: The potential (fortunately, never realized) for the dominant food system to crash and burn; the resilience of a local food system and the ability of major institutions to adjust in a crisis.

We are now swamped by a microscopic virus whose backlit photos suggest an organism of luminous beauty rather than one of mass destruction. In a manner not unlike the "cocooning" that we employed during the aftershock of 9/11, we are told to self-quarantine, social distance, and shelter-in-place by public health folks whom we now lean on the way a drunk leans on a lamp post. During 9/11, almost nineteen years ago, we watched in horror as a massive plume of black smoke carried the molecules of thousands of lost souls into the skies over metro New York City, soon to waft, serene as a host of angels, over the Atlantic Ocean. Clinging together desperately against the incomprehensible chaos, we never found an answer to our collective question of "why?" Many of us drowned in grief, some were shocked into silence, others marched off to the nearest military recruiting station like their grandfathers had in the days following the attack on Pearl Harbor.

Lacking an obvious foe—Al Qaeda terrorists or Japanese militarists—we may be even more stunned by the onslaught of the coronavirus, today's "enemy" whose source—metaphysical and physical—seems uncertain at best and against which we cannot send bombers or battalions of young men and women. Hunkering down, closing down, and canceling all that propels our reason for living are anathema to our social natures which cry out for engagement, revenge, and reassertion of a dignity now denied by something absolutely unseen. Our leaders do their best to gird our loins for a passive war even when our first response is to attack, not to seek cover.

Standing down from the things we love in times of a pandemic—the company of others, good food and beverage, my eight now canceled spring speaking engagements—frustrates the pursuit of passions we hold dear. In Nobel Prize winning author Gabriel García Márquez' *Love in the Time of Cholera* we recognize that the Spanish meaning for cholera (colera) is as much anger and passion as it is a disease. The novel's characters struggle with overwhelming amorous feelings held against a backdrop of a country-consuming illness. As we navigate our way through a public health crisis not seen since the early days of the Aids/HIV epidemic, our success or failure this time around, as it was with 9/11, will rest on how we find new but challenging ways to love in the face of the indifferent disease.

The Farmers' Market

Using her latex-gloved hand, the farmer gently moves my grasping paw away from the neatly stacked heads of lettuce. I realized this was no longer the good old farmers' market days of picking through the bins or holding the apples up for inspection. The Santa Fe Farmers' Market is now practicing safe shopping—instead of "pick your own" we're now doing "you point, I'll pick." This Saturday's winter market was missing one-third of its normal vendors and the crowd was down by that much as well. While people seemed a bit nervous—6-feet distance between customers being impossible to maintain at a farmers' market—they were happy to be there, reassured perhaps that some farmers were willing to show up. After all, we were more secure here than we would be at the area's supermarkets whose aisles were packed to the gills with tense shoppers pushing bulging carts. There was no hoarding at the market, just soft murmurings between friends about those "local meals" they were making at home that evening since their favorite farm to table restaurant was closed for the duration.

You never have to look too far to always find a tidbit of good news at the farmers' market. Today's pleasant surprise was that the "Honey Man" was back after his successful rotator cuff surgery over the winter. Believe me, rumors were flying that his return was uncertain, which is the kind of gossip that can send shock waves through the faithful. His reappearance alongside beautiful brown quarts of "Bucking Bee Honey" squelched the upsetting noise of rumormongers, thus stabilizing global honey markets, or at least the part of the globe that is Santa Fe. Remember, several farmers' trucks and their goods were lost beneath the rubble of the World Trade Center on 9/11, while millions of dollars in lost market sales followed in its aftermath at the peak of the Northeast harvest season. Our support (and love) for farmers is as necessary now as then.

Your farmers' market is just one of many small candles burning against the darkness. The mutual assistance initiatives cropping up like crocuses are another as neighbors and youth groups organize themselves to deliver food to those who must self-quarantine, or to form phone-trees that will conduct wellness checks. Keeping our farmers in business is obviously important, but so are the numerous other small businesses and individual entrepreneurs who are essential to our communities. One Santa Fe writer offered tips for how to keep a local, independent book store operational even though it must close its doors for now. Two things you can do, he suggested, are to buy coupons from the store now that can be used to make purchases in the future, and to order books directly from the store that they in turn will order for you from their suppliers.

Friends from Jacksonville, Florida (see my new book *Food Town, USA*, 2019) report on the efforts of the Northeast Florida Food Bank to feed their hungry clients. The dire news coming from food banks is that the quantity of food donated by retailers through normal weekly food recovery programs and processes is diminishing. Just as consumers are experiencing empty shelves at their local grocery stores, those same stores are reducing the amount of product to pull from their shelves at night for donation to the food bank. This is forcing food banks to source paid products to replace any potential shortfall, which means they need cash donations. Food banks are the feeder of last resort for many Americans. This may be a good time to dig a little deeper into your charitable piggy bank.

Likewise, the Northeast Florida Food Bank has experienced an 80 to 90 percent reduction in the number of volunteers due to cancelations amid health concerns. They state that, "We are actively seeking more volunteers in the short term while staying within the following guidelines: Maximum of thirty volunteers per volunteer shift, age restrictions, and responding to health screening questions prior to entering the warehouse." Stepping outside of our immediate comfort/safety zone within an acceptable range of risk may be necessary to fulfill our obligation to take care of our own.

My son, Peter, both a horticulturalist and musician, offers this advice to keep both the creative and brewing classes afloat:

> I've spent a lot of my life dependent on income from professions that revolve around public gatherings (mostly music). Though that's not the case for me now, my heart aches for my many friends who still are. Please remember there are ways to support them that don't require public gatherings. Buy a local artist's album on Bandcamp. Or pick up their LP and have a couple of friends over for a listening party. Grab a six-pack from a local brewery even if you can't stop by their tasting room. And if the going gets real tough, support their crowd funding requests.

Take care of the artists, the small business owners, and all the other weirdos who sacrificed reliable incomes (and often health insurance) to make this world a more creative and dynamic place for the rest of us.

I remain, as I probably always will, a snarling mass of contradiction who'd sooner wear the tattered rags of opposition than don the cloak of stoicism. But when I give myself permission to breathe deeply, to use this good brain that God gave me, I see more clearly the things over which I can gain control, as well as the things that I cannot. Little is accomplished stressing over the numerous lost speaking gigs that I had prepared so hard for, whose notes, data, jokes, PowerPoints, and practiced facial expressions are now no more than part of a gathering plume of smoke blocking out the sun. After all, the calendar tells me, as does the subtle shift in temperature, that spring is on the land. Better to assert my voice through my too-soft hands and aging back than waste visceral energy on that which has evaporated in the wink of an eye.

Therefore, I have resolved this season to grow the best fucking garden ever! To that end I have expanded my raised bed space by 50 percent, amped up my Johnny's Seed Catalog order, and just finished loading and unloading 400 pounds of bagged, composted manure. The hardworking, fast moving young man at the Lowes Garden Center who helped me with the manure told me that, "It's crazy around here. We're all running because business is up 13 percent this week." When I asked him what they were selling, he said, "Freezers." Well, I thought, I'm working the production end of the food chain where I'll grow enough for me, my neighbors, and even the food pantry. I'm not taking a survivalist, store and hoard, shelter-in-place approach. I'm attacking this "enemy" head on with my rake, hoe, and wheelbarrow.

I will urge the same upon you, my friends. The times, the circumstances, and the soft scent of spring call us to join a campaign that we might anoint, "Victory Garden 2020." Let's fight back against the pandemic by digging and planting as much good earth as we can, household by household, community garden plot by community garden plot, window box by window box. The love of our land, the love of good food, and the love for each other, shared with heart and muscle, will win the struggle.

CHAPTER TWENTY

The Poetry of Community Food Assessments

April, 2014

This is my "treatise" on the role that imagination should play in shaping one's community research and response methodology. I place an emphasis on slow and careful observation and a sustained and non-invasive presence. The so-called facts of a place and its challenges are not only contained in bits of data. They are revealed in the personality of individuals, their relationship to others in their community, and the historical influence of both past and present institutions. The sense of this essay is not limited to research or simply gaining an understanding on how to proceed in any given place, it is also intended as a prescription for life, especially if one's life work carries with it a commitment to seeking justice and reducing inequality, whether professionally or personally. Biggest surprise: Poetry can be as useful a teacher for community work as it can be for how we live our everyday lives and interact with the world around us.

How has our approach to understanding community food systems become like our approach to poetry? I took some instruction recently from former US Poet Laureate, Billy Collins who asks his students "to take a poem and hold it up to the light." He wants them to sit with it for a while, enjoy its many features and nuances, and slowly absorb feelings and meanings. Perhaps out of an earnest attempt to please the teacher and finish the assignment, they "tie the poem to a chair ... /And torture a confession out of it."

The more I see of community food assessments—a process whereby researchers and stakeholders gather information about their food system in order to better understand its strengths and weaknesses—the more I worry that, like Collins's over-zealous students, we are torturing the subject while never getting to know its essence.

Though there are limits in comparing a food system to a poem, I find more similarities than not in our reliance on quantitative techniques and an obsession with wrestling the "facts" to the ground. Like the innocent poem that is pressed against a slide for unrelenting dissection, we are too often launching waves of graduate student drones over target zones, laptops programmed and grids drawn. Couldn't we float and flit for a bit, and like butterflies that light on meadow flora, sniff, touch, and taste the place for a while? I like to look at my surroundings through different lenses, hold them up for scrutiny in varying lights, and put my ear to the hive to check the buzz. When it comes to the community food assessments, we're too much above it all and over-fueled with high-octane, evidence-based objectivity. The truth is on the ground where we are.

Just as the imaginative reader of a poem holds hands with the lines and images until the molecules are absorbed through his skin, the food system investigator who opens up her sociological imagination might discover something unique, beautiful, and, yes, often deeply disturbing. Instead of inducing rigor mortis with scientific rigor, as I have seen some community food assessments do, why not let the assessment process unfold slowly, even over a lifetime, by simply making it an everyday occurrence? And by "a lifetime" I certainly don't mean that we twiddle our thumbs, waiting, as some groups have, for the data to tell them what to do. As a community food activist who should be immersed in your place, you will always be searching, asking questions, and keeping your ear pressed gently to the ground.

It was sometime after my fifteenth year of running the Hartford Food System before I felt like I understood what was going on in that city and the state of Connecticut. We had learned from firsthand experience, later backed up by surveys, that Hartford's food was more expensive than that in the suburbs; we discovered that the city's bus routes didn't take people to supermarkets that had fled to the suburbs; we found, after watching farms disappear for a decade, that Connecticut was losing farmland faster than anywhere else in the nation. With a prima facie case in hand, we swooped in, gathered more evidence, secured an indictment, and started the corrections job as fast as possible. But it took fifteen years of living and working in a place—looking under the hood and scraping our shins on the truth—before we got it.

I want science to be ruthlessly rigorous when searching for links between tobacco and lung cancer, or factory livestock operations and antibiotic resistance, but when it comes to understanding the community experience, something softer is called for, something perhaps more intuitive and anthropological. You see, our imagination is central to our work. Without it we never would have conceived of this thing we call a food system in the first place. The connections between food, health, environment; the idea of a feeding web; even ideas like social capital and community would have remained isolated within their own disciplinary boxes if we hadn't sought a bigger horizon, one not constrained by reductionist thinking. While I may be quirky in finding beauty in a food system, I do believe we all find joy and satisfaction in discovering the connection between two or more previously disparate things.

When it comes to how we assess a community's food system, listening is the most important tool we have. I was reminded of this at a recent Santa Fe Food Policy Council meeting where we were discussing our food assessment and draft food plan. One member of the community had come to the meeting to put forward some unsolicited ideas. But, according to our public testimony rules, we could only grant her two minutes to speak, much of which was consumed by her trying to keep her two overactive young children from disassembling the muffin tray. Frustrated and pissed, she corralled me afterwards in the parking lot where she went on at some length saying, "if you want the public there, if you want poor people there, you better have child care ..." I listened hard; I agreed with her, and tried to relate and repeat what she said. I suggested that she set up a neighborhood meeting where we could discuss the food plan and hear her neighbors' thoughts. She is now organizing that gathering.

Time is a great oppressor, a dictator that truncates the human experience to digestible data bits and highly efficient exchanges—life reduced to a hashtag. Our task is to slow down and slow dance, make eye contact, and, when necessary, give ourselves a wide berth from the rules, the clock, and the agenda. As the Zen master Yogi Berra once said, "You can observe a lot by watchin'."

C. Wright Mills, the great lefty sociologist and Columbia University professor may have written one of the best treatises on social science methodology: *The Sociological Imagination.* Published in 1959, it is worthy of a read by all food system researchers, assessors, and activists. Mills was an advocate of a more values-based approach to social science research and an early critic of the statistical slavery that was then overtaking his field. In one lashing he wrote, "The 'empirical facts' are facts collected by a bureaucratically guided set of usually semi-skilled individuals. It has been forgotten that social observation requires high skill and acute sensibility; that discovery often occurs precisely when an imaginative mind sets itself down in the middle of social realities." While being overly harsh toward those we depend on for numbers, I have little doubt that Mills would agree with Billy Collins that a poetic sensibility and a sociological imagination are kissing cousins.

When I see our earnest food assessors serving their method before their community, I recall my favorite Mills's admonishment: "Many ... social scientists in America today ... conform to the prevailing fear of any passionate commitment." Trembling, unsure of which God they serve, the best and the brightest too often balk because the data have not reached their desired level of perfection—a bar they always push higher and often never climb over.

While the threats to our food system are far too urgent for us to succumb entirely to the sweet indulgence of poetry, I think there are lessons to be learned from those who desire more profound ways of understanding. If a poem sends an unfamiliar surge up my spine—whether disturbing or pleasurable—it has done its job, and I am now in a heightened state of readiness. While discussions of syntax, meter, and the poet's sexual preference may provide a minimal amount of illumination, it is the generous beat of the poetic sensibility that is the true torch.

To what end do we seek a better understanding of our food system? I suspect that it is for reasons more profound than simply producing the interventions that may follow. For if we have succeeded in establishing a food hub, or getting another serving of local vegetables on a cafeteria tray, have we truly done all that can be done? If today's industrial food system is guilty, as I believe it is, of feeding consumers to maintain their status as, what Mills calls "Cheerful Robots," do we food advocates necessarily offer a qualitatively better experience?

It seems that the task of any inquiry, including a community food assessment, should be the elevation of the human condition, not only through the addition of more and better goods and services, but also by contributing to the growth of individual freedom and reason. "Freedom" as Mills says, "is the chance to formulate the available choices ... and then the opportunity to choose," a process that cannot occur without an enlargement in human reason. Spending more time interacting with people and their place—not just more time refining the data—will enlarge everyone's reason. This may make our work of understanding a food system a more difficult and longer enterprise, but it will make it richer, more enjoyable, and, in the long run, significantly more rewarding.

CHAPTER TWENTY-ONE

Food Co-ops: A Faith Renewed

June, 2013

Cooperatives—ownership by the members and profits distributed to the members and/or plowed back into the business—have been both an affirmative lifestyle choice by those who believe in their ideals as much as they have been a response to food system and marketplace failures. Whether they are farmers banding together in an effort to control the price they receive for their products or consumers seeking to fill an empty food desert with affordable, high-quality food, co-ops set about the task of meeting people's needs first rather than those of corporate shareholders or private investors. Over recent years, a steady resurgence in retail food co-ops has filled the marketplace gaps created by the abandonment of many communities by the supermarket industry. While the development of these enterprises is demanding, and the timeframes unusually long, they clearly represent community collaboration at its best in their attempt to respond to serious flaws in the capitalist economy. Biggest surprise: Food co-ops work!

"FAITH IS A STRAY PET THAT WILL SOMEHOW FIND YOU AGAIN."
DAVID HERNANDEZ, POET

For the better part of forty years, my fondest memory of retail food co-ops was the day they closed. Even though my heart was broken, the handwritten "Out of Bizness" sign hung from the ill-fated venture's front door signaled the end of my misery and the first day of the rest my life. With a faith born out of an over-heated idealism, I had sacrificed a living, a bit of my health, and no small part of my soul to the notion that funky storefront co-ops could ride like the cavalry to the rescue of supermarket-abandoned communities and those seeking high-quality food. With the store's end a painful certainty, I could now retreat into rehab to recover my sanity.

That's why it felt like some form of divine intervention when I received the invitation to speak at this year's Consumer Cooperative Management Association (CCMA) conference in Austin. While I no longer broke out in hives when someone asked me about co-ops, I couldn't help but wonder if I was being called back to a church I had long since slammed the door on. Either way, I could hardly address 400 retail food co-op managers and board members with a bad attitude, or like the angry Presbyterian ministers of my youth, chastise them for failing to solve all of America's food problems.

As it turned out, and as my research turned up, my path to co-op redemption was far easier than I thought. No longer operating out of the back of your neighbor's garage, co-op food stores are full-fledged business enterprises, managed by a professional staff, and generally well capitalized. They are not necessarily single-store operations either. The Puget Consumer Co-op (PCC) in Seattle has ten stores with an eleventh on the way. La Montanita in New Mexico has five stores with a sixth expected within the year. And annual sales are also nothing to sneeze at. The Park Slope Food Co-op in Brooklyn has 16,000 members and $48 million in annual sales. Burlington, Vermont's City Market-Onion River Co-op has 8,000 members and $33 million in sales. Nationwide, combined co-op sales are in the billions and official membership exceeds 1.3 million.

But it's not only their growth and impressive business performance that distinguishes co-ops; it's their adherence to a set of inviolate principles that have also made them successful social enterprises. In the course of my research and interaction with CCMA conference goers, I came across amazing stories of true democracy in the workplace and marketplace, efforts to educate and inform eaters, initiatives to reduce hunger, and strategies to develop regional agriculture and resilient communities.

Like food co-ops everywhere, the Good Foods Co-op in Lexington, Kentucky holds firm to the principles of open membership, democratic control, member ownership and financing, community concern, equality, equity, and solidarity. Growing since 1972, Good Foods now occupies a lovely 12,000-square-foot space that I had the privilege to visit a year ago. In addition to selling great food, the co-op makes monthly donations to local non-profits, assists a local food pantry, and participates in nutrition and health programs.

Thanks to a survey of co-op activity by Darrow Vanderburg-Wertz, I learned how co-ops are reaching out to their community's low-income residents. The City Market-Onion River Co-op in Burlington accepts SNAP and WIC benefits, which represent about $1.3 million of their $33 million in annual sales; has volunteer work options that allow discounts on purchases; makes free deliveries to senior housing complexes; offers free cooking classes to discounted members; and partners with the state WIC program to offer frugal shopping and basic cooking programs, which includes incentive gift cards to encourage WIC participants to shop at the co-op.

The spirit of co-ops and their promise to rejuvenate economically depressed communities is alive and well in Dorchester, MA where citizens and members recently raised $26,000 toward their new store. They now have almost 300 members and, building off a successful community garden and farmers' market, have started a $2 million capital campaign to build out a space for a co-op food store in an area that can only be called a food desert (see update). And according to Joe Amedeo, board member of the newly founded Bethlehem (Pennsylvania) Food Co-op, work is underway to bring a co-op to a couple of food desert communities in that former steel city's downtown.

And co-ops aren't just for urban areas. The Dixon Food Co-op has been open since 2005 in Dixon, New Mexico, a town of only 2,000 people. Its development was assisted by a USDA Community

Food Projects grant. In Orange, Massachusetts, an old New England mill town where the mills have long since disappeared, the Quabbin Harvest Co-op has been serving that small town for over ten years.

My "hometown co-op," La Montanita, is New Mexico's leader in buying and distributing local food. Through their warehousing, local business investment programs, and extended partnerships, including an innovative mobile grocery program operating in vast and sparsely populated Native American Pueblos, they are sourcing 1,100 local products from 400 local producers, which now represent 20 percent of their co-op's sales.

I learned from the Sacramento and Davis Food Co-ops that co-ops aren't just interested in buying local, they want to ensure that there will be a local to buy from. Through a member-supported effort, the two co-ops are raising funds to purchase an easement on the Central Valley organic farm owned by Jeff and Annie Main. A documentary film *The Last Crop*, that tells the story of the farm and the co-ops' efforts to preserve it, is in the making. Once the funds are raised—not a foregone conclusion but certainly a likely one—the farm will be farmed in perpetuity and the co-ops will have astutely protected a portion of their food supply.

From a fine paper written by Byrd and Winston that compared food co-ops to Walmart, I was reminded of the extraordinary history and work of New Hampshire's Hanover Co-op, started in 1936. The co-op recently intervened to take over a failed independent grocer in the lower middle-income town of White River Junction, Vermont. In spite of the high risk associated with re-opening a store in this area, the co-op saw an opportunity to sell high-quality food at low prices to people who needed both. The co-op saved jobs, expanded the market for local food, improved the local economy by keeping more food dollars in the community, and earned an enormous amount of goodwill.

While not every member of the Hanover Co-op embraced this investment, one board member told me that, "yes, we could have used our profits to give our members lower prices, but chose instead to open a store in a community that needed one." A similar sentiment was echoed by a PCC board member who said that the co-op is solicited all the time by affluent Seattle area neighborhoods that want a PCC store, but their new store will open in a lower income community for three reasons: the success of their earlier stores gave them the necessary resources to assume a modest level of risk; the new store is projected to be financially successful; and their values dictate that a needier neighborhood should come first.

How do co-ops compare overall to Walmart and other conventional supermarkets? Food co-ops spend 38 percent of their revenues locally compared to 24 percent by conventional grocers; source 20 percent of their products locally compared to 6 percent; keep 17 percent more money in the community; sell 82 percent of their produce as organic compared to 12 percent, and create significantly more full-time jobs with benefits.

Now, I do find that I spend more money for food at my co-op than I do for comparable items at an Albertson's Supermarket. But I know that every extra dime I spend is being reinvested in the co-op, going back to members, paying workers a living wage and decent benefits, buying from local farmers, and strengthening the economic underpinnings of my community. Can Albertson's or Walmart make those claims?

Given the extraordinary commitment to community development by the retail co-op movement over the past decade, you have to wonder why the Obama administration turned to Walmart to restore America's food deserts. It's highly likely that a modest public investment by the federal government (and states as well) in a co-op-oriented food store development strategy would achieve a higher rate of return to community equity, workers, regional agriculture, and healthier food, to say nothing of citizen democracy!

But therein lies the rub, and I think the promise as well, that co-ops can and should play a much larger role in the rejuvenation of our local and regional food systems. Like a lantern under a bushel basket, co-ops only burn bright for the limited number of eyes that can see them. A bigger noise and a broader beam are called for, ones that could be projected far and wide if the millions of co-op members and shoppers rolled up their sleeves and became politically active.

Co-ops aren't by any means neophytes in the world of public policy. They've been on the frontlines in the state and federal battles to label genetically engineered food, for instance. But imagine one million co-op members getting severely agitated about food insecurity, poverty and the nation's wealth gap, and the growing unsustainability of our food system. Congress would listen, state legislatures would listen, and the general public would not only perk up, it might even buy a co-op membership.

Yes, my faith in co-ops as a force for community-level change has been restored. But the time has come for co-ops to take what they've done so well, albeit on a smaller scale, and go big, get loud, and show the country that cooperative development just might be the ticket to social justice and a democratically controlled food system.

Update: The Dorchester Food Co-op officially opened its doors in October 2023 after nearly fourteen years of organizing and development work. As of early 2024, it had over 2,000 dues-paying members. It also received development assistance from the USDA Community Food Projects Competitive Grant Program. "Grocery Co-op USA" says that—combined co-op sales nationally are $2.4 billion. A 2023 "Food Co-op Impact Report" produced by the National Grocers Association identified 239 co-ops in thirty-nine states, however, a quick review of their data found several co-ops unreported including the Dixon, NM, and Dorchester, MA co-ops.

CHAPTER TWENTY-TWO

Twenty-Five Years of Food Security, Good Food, and Empowerment

June, 2021

The manner in which a community comes together to reduce food insecurity is always a source of fascination. Sometimes the efforts are designed to meet the immediate needs of vulnerable households, but other times, as in the case to follow, we see more systemic and sustainable responses that push back against inequality and produce results that extend far beyond the provision of food. Such responses require a bigger vision and a core of creativity that's capable of imagining how one action connects to the next, and how multiple results can be produced by a single intervention. While a spark of innovation is necessary to ignite the kindling, it often requires a healthy dose of public policy and subsequent government funding to fan the flames of deep change. Biggest surprise: The power of one small grant program to render such a long-term and sustainable change.

The anchor institution for this small western city is the University of Montana, well known among its other academic departments, for its forestry and sustainability programs in a region that *had* been known for agriculture. As the end the twentieth century approached, the story of American food production was one of a declining number of farms, the survivors of which were growing ever larger by consolidating with other farms and producing commodity crops for global markets. That trend left regions of the country, like the one Missoula inhabited, disappearing in agriculture's rearview mirror. After all, who needs to grow food for their own region when the glittering lights of "Big Food" beckon and gleaming, one-size-fits-all supermarkets provide for everyone's needs?

As it turns out, there was a parallel food narrative strongly suggesting that not everyone's food needs were being met. A decade's worth of cuts in the nation's safety net programs accompanied by the falling value of wages relative to the cost of living—the early signs of growing income inequality—revealed themselves in USDA's first surveys of food insecurity among US households. Depending on a number of factors and the particular year, anywhere from one in ten to one in six Americans faced food insecurity. This led to another disquieting trend, namely the growth in food pantries and food banks that grew in size and number in response to the increased demand for free food. This unfolding crisis, a foreshadowing of crises to come including the impact of the coronavirus pandemic, pushed thousands of communities back on their heels as they scavenged for local solutions.

"I was working at the Missoula Food Bank at that time," said Bonnie Buckingham, long-time area resident and now the director of the Community Food and Agriculture Coalition, "when Josh Slotnick walked in with an idea. He wanted to grow food on some vacant land for the food bank." In 1996, with two acres of donated land, Josh, a young but landless farmer, and a number of volunteers, students, and the university, started what would come to be known as the PEAS Farm. Even twenty-five years later, Bonnie remembers how excited she was when "2,000 pounds of amazing sustainably grown produce" showed up in the food bank's warehouse that season.

But PEAS Farm wasn't just a "one-off" attempt to close the local food gap. It was the beginning of what soon became the non-profit organization, Garden City Harvest (GCH) that got its financial start with a $50,000 grant from the brand new, USDA Community Food Projects Competitive Grant Program. Better known as "CFP," the federal program's thirteen original 1996 grant recipients included GCH, and since that grant coincided with the organization's founding, both GCH and CFP are celebrating their twenty-fifth anniversaries in 2021.

"GCH is now an essential part of Missoula," Bonnie told me. This is a statement that precisely reflects the intention of CFP, which is now administered by USDA's National Institute of Food and Agriculture (NIFA), formerly the Cooperative State Research, Education, and Extension Service (CSREES). Based on the program's own grant application language, applicants will be required to demonstrate that their projects "increase the self-reliance of communities in providing for their own food needs ... plan for long-term solutions ... create innovative marketing activities that mutually benefit agricultural producers and low-income consumers." There is no better evidence of what these achievements look like today than in GCH's current line-up of activities: four neighborhood farms and eleven community garden sites that serve nearly 400 gardeners; 290 community supported agriculture shares; a robust farm to school and school garden program that serves thousands of school-age children every year. Not only is their food production output envious—over one-quarter of a million pounds are grown and distributed annually—they touch the lives of nearly everybody in Missoula. Reviewing those twenty-five years, Bonnie said "Not only was GHC visionary and innovative, it has raised the potential for western Montana to feed itself."

The CFP grew out of efforts by the Community Food Security Coalition (CFSC), which itself was inspired by the principles of community food security. Recognizing that the success of local efforts to end hunger, reduce obesity, and promote sustainable food and farming economies was dependent on a food systems approach—acknowledging the relationship between all the parts of a food system, from seed to table (and now waste, the environment, and health)—CFSC felt that one way to advance community food security was through a dedicated federal grant program.

As an emerging food and farm coalition, CFSC and its members launched a number of initiatives in the mid- to late-1990s to support the work of grassroots people and organizations that were committed to more holistic and justice-oriented approaches. But without the recognition and resources that federal policy provides, the ability to catalyze a community-based food movement would be a slow, hard slog. With the assistance of numerous supporters, both at the local level and on Capitol Hill, CFSC and its allies advocated for inclusion of a community-oriented federal grant program that would empower local food system stakeholders to choose their own path to food security and sustainability. Key among its congressional supporters were Julie Paradis, ranking staff member of the House Agriculture Committee, and Representatives Bill Emerson of Missouri and Eligio "Kika" de la Garza of Texas.

Looking back on that period in the mid-1990s, it's important to note how unique and innovative the CFP concept was compared to other very large federal food programs like food stamps and commodity support programs for agriculture. De la Garza said it best when introducing the bill that would later become the Community Food Projects Competitive Grant Program: "The concept of community food security is a comprehensive strategy for feeding hungry people, one that incorporates the participation of the community and encourages a greater role for the entire food system ... There is a need to develop innovative approaches ... that foster local solutions and that deliver multiple benefits to communities."

With its emphasis on community participation and decision-making—what today goes by such terms as "food democracy" and "food sovereignty"—CFP not only set the stage for a host of other locally focused food programs, like FINI/GusNIP and the FMLFPP, but gave communities an alternative to bureaucratic-heavy, top-down, and charity-driven hunger mitigation strategies. It has paved the way through nearly 650 grants totaling more than $100 million to all US states and territories, for a deeper dive into the underlying causes of our nation's food problems. In turn, CFP unleashed a panoply of creative organizational and individual responses to America's food security and sustainability challenges.

Josh Slotnick moved on from farming and GCH about three years ago and eventually become a Missoula County commissioner. In his twenty-two years at GCH, he expanded the PEAS Farm from two to ten acres and helped to grow the organization overall. Jean Zosel was hired as GCH's executive director ten years ago. According to Jean, GCH now has twenty-one sites totaling more than twenty acres throughout the community, including four acres that it purchased and that serve as GHC's hub. There's an office, a community barn and kitchen, an apartment for the farm's caretaker, and an orchard, in addition to other farming and gardening areas.

Over the course of expanding and diversifying their activities over the past decades, Jean makes it clear that they stayed true to their mission, one that she fully credits Josh for embedding in the community. "Addressing food insecurity is in our DNA," she said, noting among other facts that 70 percent of their community gardeners are low to moderate income and that a substantial amount of their community farm production (20,000 pounds of produce a year) still goes to the food bank. But over the past fifteen months, GCH proved its mettle by providing a readily accessible and affordable source of local food during the pandemic. "Boy, oh boy! Growing food was a big deal last year," she exclaimed, telling me that all the CSA shares sold out for the first time ever and its community garden sites generated long waiting lists.

Not to downplay the impact of the pandemic or the role that GCH played in stepping up to the plate, Jean says, "we were created [in 1996] in response to a crisis, so our response to the pandemic was just part of our job. After all, there are always people in our community living in crisis." But both Jean and Bonnie reserve their greatest enthusiasm for what might be considered the least quantifiable or tangible influences of GCH. "We have literally grown thousands of environmental stewards," Jean said, referring to about 1,200 University of Montana Environmental Studies students who have cycled through GCH over the past twenty-five years, as well as the 6,500 public school kids who annually experience a variety a food and farm activities.

The community connections are infinite, and that so many of them can be attributed to food, Missoula's two farmers' markets, and GCH are undeniable. They are as unique and individual to Missoula as they are common to communities across the country. One small example that Jean cites concerns GCH's youth-run, mobile market that sells their low-cost, sustainably grown produce to Missoula's senior citizens. "These are young people who usually occupy Missoula's margins," she told me. "They are socially isolated but seem to connect with seniors who are also socially isolated. One of our young women told me, 'I've got purple hair, and let's face it, this is not normal. But the seniors think I'm wonderful!'"

Twenty-five years of tons of locally grown food, thousands of young people launched like bees across the community and countryside to pollinate sustainable agriculture and community food security projects elsewhere, and uncountable personal interactions that have enriched people's lives in unimaginable ways are just some of the legacies of Garden City Harvest and Community Food Projects.

CHAPTER TWENTY-THREE

The Most Important Word in "Community Gardening" is not "Gardening"!

August, 2017

In many ways urban agriculture, which includes community gardening, has been highly underrated by those who perceive it as a redundant if not useless drop in a greater food system sea. As a net contribution to the nation's total food supply there may be some truth to that. But when the analysis takes into account the larger social, geographic, economic, and environmental impacts of smaller scale, close-in land cultivation and food production, a different picture emerges. It's potential to shrink inequality, build food security, and promote sustainability, to saying nothing of how it supports mental hygiene have typically been underrated or ignored. Biggest surprise: I have cultivated at least fifteen gardens in my lifetime. The one urban garden I tilled for several years had the best soil I've ever seen!

I've always loved community gardens because they come in such a variety of shapes and sizes. You can find them tucked into the oddest places like a pie-shaped city block, on the apron of an airport runway, or in the middle of a forgotten vacant lot. Due perhaps to my peculiar landscape aesthetic, I was very happy to give this year's keynote at the Thirty-eighth Annual American Community Gardening Association Conference in my former hometown of Hartford, Connecticut.

Almost 200 people gathered from across the country to explore and share the near-infinite ways we have contrived to cultivate "a comfortable subsistence from the smallest area of soil," to use Abraham Lincoln's words. The workshops were as intriguing as the enthusiasm was palpable as the variations were fantastical! So, let me share an excerpted version of the keynote I gave to these noble gardeners, all of whom had the best dirt I've ever seen lodged 'neath their nails.

ACGA Annual Conference 2017 Keynote

Community gardening and urban agriculture play important roles in promoting food security, healthy eating, and a sustainable and equitable food system. For those reasons, I'm going to use my time today to explore three myths that are part of the community gardening conversation.

Myth Number One: Community gardening nurtures human tranquility, a oneness with nature, and a reduction in stress. Myth Number Two: Urban gardens and farms will feed a hungry world and create a slew of good-paying jobs to boot. Myth Number Three: These gardeners and farmers exist in such a singular state of purity and righteousness that they can float above the political fray eschewing any serious engagement with public policy.

Let's dispense with the first myth—the supernatural power of community gardening to assuage the anxieties of modern life. When I lived in Hartford, I was a member of the Watkinson Community Garden. I loved going there because the 100 or so plots adjoined meadows and the Park River that were home to cardinals, finches, orioles, bluebirds, and swallows. The river banks were alive with muskrats, snakes, and the occasional skunk. Deer would sometimes vault the garden's fence to dine on a few heads of lettuce.

But early one June, a gardener discovered a large woodchuck had taken up residence inside the garden and was munching on everything he could get his little paws on. The men mobilized immediately with the precision of a military unit. Three volunteers went on reconnaissance to locate each of the interloper's points of access and egress where they stood watch with hoes and shovels at the ready. The platoon commander, carrying a gasoline canister, found the chuck's main entrance to his den and filled it with petrol. Yelling "fire in the hole!" he dropped a full book of lit matches into the now saturated warren sending a fireball twenty-feet into the air, which threw the gardener/warrior onto his back. The singed, but still agile chuck darted for his life from one of his exits only to be greeted by shovel-wielding gardeners whose tools—plowshares now turned into weapons—soon dispatched the poor fellow in a most unsavory manner.

Murder and mayhem in the community garden; the finches and bluebirds sought refuge in a nearby housing project; man's dominance over nature was restored, but tranquility came to a grinding halt.

A recent *New York Times* article stated that, "If you're a human being living in 2017 and you're not anxious, there's something wrong with you." Our children are over-scheduled and over-stimulated by "jiu-jitsu lessons, clarinet practice, and Advance Placement tutoring," and their iPhones are surgically attached to their wrists. No wonder, according to the same article, that 36 percent of girls and 26 percent of boys between the ages of thirteen and seventeen suffer from anxiety disorder. Anxiety fuels marijuana purchases that are now a $6.7 billion industry. Those who voted for Trump did so because they were anxious; those who did not are now extremely anxious.

If we're going to boast about the paradisiacal qualities of community gardens, we need to ensure that they live up to our hopes. Now more than ever, the world needs to slow down and sniff the zucchini blossoms, take a Zen-walk along garden paths, and savor the deliciousness of the productions of the earth.

Myth Number Two: Urban gardens and farms will feed a hungry world and create a slew of good-paying jobs. First, let's be clear about the cause of hunger and food insecurity. It is poverty, which is itself fueled by America's enormous wealth and income disparities, particularly low wages. The stark facts are these:

- The US leads the developed world in income inequality.
- The top 1 percent took in 19 percent of all income while the 10 percent took in 48 percent.
- 70 percent of all private wealth is held by the top 10 percent while the 1 percent control 35 percent.

These numbers are hideous and won't be altered by community gardens nor anything other than a radical restructuring of our tax code. They need our immediate attention, and I hope the voices of community gardeners join those who hunger for social and economic equality.

My colleagues at the Johns Hopkins Center for a Livable Future looked at the benefits associated with urban agriculture for a bill that Senator Debbie Stabenow was working on. They combed through the literature, and, based on the evidence, they found that urban agriculture:

- Significantly increases social capital, community well-being, and civic engagement.
- Provides a number of ecosystem services to urban areas, e.g., one pound of food production displaces two pounds of carbon.
- Supports participants' physical and psychosocial health.
- Supplements household food security.
- Is associated with increased property values.
- Offers opportunities for skills development, workforce training, and supplemental income (these benefits normally require subsidies to achieve).

In sum, however, no large-scale job creation benefits could be demonstrated.

That being said, there is evidence that gardens are associated with obesity reduction and better health outcomes, and reduce crime and municipal maintenance costs. Even though community gardens and small urban farms are not big food contributors, 30 percent of US agriculture production occurs in metro areas.

Of course, skeptics abound. Spokespersons for Big Farming have turned their noses up at these so-called "urban aesthetes" and "utopian farmers" whose acreage is so small it can barely support a rototiller. But with a billion of the globe's people hungry, a billion undernourished, and another billion obese, conventional and industrial forms of agriculture have hardly earned bragging rights.

Urban agriculture and community gardens may not feed a hungry world, but they certainly can feed a hungry spirit and a hunger for both natural and human connection. As the world becomes less food secure every day, growing food in unconventional places will no longer be thought of as a nicety, like a flowerbox of petunias slung from a brownstone's windowsill, but as a necessity born out of the looming realization that there will be 9 billion of us to feed by 2050. At the very least, one can think of urban farming as an insurance policy with a very small monthly premium.

Let's consider Myth Number Three: Communit gardeners and farmers exist in such a singular state of purity and righteousness that they can float above the political fray eschewing any serious engagement with public policy. Over 150 years ago, Abraham Lincoln, speaking in favor of the newly formed land grant university system and the Department of Agriculture, said, "Our population [will] increase [which makes] the most valuable of all arts ... the art of deriving a comfortable subsistence from the smallest area of soil. No community whose every member possesses this art, can ever be the victim of oppression. Such a community will be independent of crowned-kings, money kings, and land-kings."

By establishing a system of publicly financed education and technical support for agriculture, and for what would later become the epicenter of food-consumer interests, Lincoln joined the ideals of American self-reliance to the principle that our public interests could be advanced through a partnership with government.

Fast forward to the present and we see a plethora of food policy activity at the local, state, and federal levels of government. While I don't necessarily want government to lead in the area of food, I do want two things. The first is to institutionalize government's role in ensuring access to healthy and affordable food for all. In other words, food should be recognized as one critical government function. The second thing I want is for government to collaborate with private sector partners to ensure that communities, states, tribal organizations, and the nation are meeting their food-related goals.

It was for these two reasons that we established the Hartford Advisory Commission on Food Policy, a food policy council that is now the second longest continuously operating food policy council out of 250 nationwide.

You may have heard last year in Cleveland how their food policy council played a critical role in revamping the city's zoning practices to support community gardening, allowing for the backyard raising of chickens and bees, providing financial support for food-related start-ups including urban farms, and changing the city's food procurement practices to give premium pricing to food produced in or near the city.

Los Angeles has added yet another dimension to municipal support for urban farming. Their food policy council was instrumental in passing an ordinance that allows property owners to lease their land to food growers in return for tax benefits. The ordinance is designed to turn vacant pieces of land into productive urban garden, and farm plots to produce food for surrounding neighborhoods, especially lower income ones. But LA also sees this change as a way to expand green spaces, reduce blight, promote social cohesion and support economic opportunities. Here again, we see a multitude of purposes and outcomes enabled through public policy.

At the federal level, USDA's Community Food Project (CFP) grant program has funded around $100 million in community food work since its inception in 1996. I don't have the numbers, but I know that much of that spending has gone to a wide variety of community agriculture projects. It would be in the best interests of AGCA and its members to ensure the continued funding of CFP.

After policy, of course, comes collaboration. Working with other stakeholders whether through a food policy council or another collaborative mechanism is essentially how you secure more policy benefits. No matter how important you are or how necessary your organization's projects, little will change in your communities unless you collaborate *fiercely* with those who share your larger purpose of promoting food security, sustainable food systems, and healthy eating.

I know that what I'm proposing isn't easy. Building collaborations with people you don't normally work with, connecting the dots within a complicated food system, and engaging public policy at all levels are hard work and can make us very uncomfortable. But as my therapist told me, embracing your inner discomfort is a necessary precursor to change.

When we do interact with others, we need to have a clear message. Here are a few ideas I'd ask you to consider. First, community gardening, urban agriculture, and all of their amazing variations need a new name—something that conveys both the spirit of non-conventional food production, is all-encompassing, and bridges geographic differences.

Second, I think we do our cause a disservice when we overstate the benefits of community gardening—it's easy to wax poetic, I do it all the time. Gardeners aren't shy about expressing their love for plants, veggies, flowers or the implacable joy of gardening. In our writings, reports, and public testimony, however, we'd be well-served by reining in some of our exuberance in favor of a more sober rendition of community gardening's cornucopia of good outcomes. To that end, let's lean on the data, and let's encourage more research that looks at the numerous values associated with community gardening.

My message boils down to this:

- The most important word in "community gardening" is "community."

- Build on the good work you are all doing, but link arms with others recognizing that none of you have all the answers.

- Engage government; the people and the policymakers must be on the same page. This is what they call democracy, and as a citizen, that is what I signed up for.

- If you don't belong to a food policy council, join one. If you don't have one, start one.

- Create a message that unifies your work and speaks to the proven benefits of community gardening.

- Poverty is the cause of hunger; the time has come to work toward the end of income and wealth inequality.

Conclusion: The Journey Continues; The Tasks are Clear

By way of review, I preceded the re-unveiling of my selected pieces of writing with a discussion of the concept of justice, a term I assert has unintentionally been overused and become unnecessarily vague. Using John Rawls's *A Theory of Justice* as a framework, I have presented the key problems facing our food systems—food insecurity, food access and dietary health, sustainability of food producing resources, and a decline in food democracy and an intimate connection to our food—as injustices that need to be anchored to and acted upon with Rawls's "original principles" in mind. To that end, the liberties that apply to one apply to all, no exceptions. Perhaps most immediate for our purposes, we need to understand the food system's injustices as deprivations that harm the disadvantaged more than others. This requires that efforts to reform food system failures must be directed first and foremost to the disadvantaged. Furthermore, the formulation of our policies and practices must account for the needs of future generations, which makes the rise of global temperatures and the near-certainty of looming atmospheric-caused tragedies a paramount concern.

Much of what underscores the relationship between food system issues and these conceptualizations of justice are the egregious economic, social, and cultural divides that sometimes feel as if they threaten to become normalized (accepted) in today's culture. To undergird the discussion of justice I have relied heavily on Robert Putnam's work and data to illustrate the income and wealth inequalities, useful historical comparisons, and cultural evolutions, especially regarding language. To augment his work, I have taken a multi-year, deep-dive into the work of Thomas Piketty and *Capital in the Twenty-First Century*.

A thread that weaves itself tightly, though perhaps not obviously through this book is my life experience. Not counting my daily meals, food issues have probably informed almost every day of my life, either personally or professionally, frequently both, since I was eighteen. During a career that has spanned fifty-six years, I have devoted most of it to directing and working for non-profit organizations, including as a ten-year stint at one academic institution, all of which were either totally or significantly involved in food system projects, policies, education, or research. I share this not to "load my resume" for the reader's sake, but to position myself as both a lifetime participant and observer of the places, people, and actions that I have addressed here. What I have attempted to draw out in my essays are portraits informed and enhanced by my experiences. I don't do this to suggest that the reader follow in my footsteps, but simply to invite you to trust and uphold the value of your own experience as you pursue the broader justice issues of the day, whether as a professional, activist, or simply an informed citizen.

The sprinkling of poetic references and lines across my pages is meant to stress the importance of the human imagination to the task at hand. Poetry, like good fiction, enables us to feel more intensely realities and impulses that are genuinely human—feelings that we are often cut off from over the course of our mundane comings and goings. We are awakened to the joy and beauty inherent in us by a scene, nature, as well as other people and places. As the philosopher Charles Taylor describes it, "a poem intensely concentrates how a given scene, or being in a given space, moves us ... [for] a heightening of awareness and a sharpening of focus." Poetry has the power to open our consciousness to original ways of seeing, doing, and especially connecting. Poetry also reduces the distance between us and the object of our interest—the closer we are to that object, the better we'll understand it. No matter how one pursues justice, and regardless of where one enters the road to a hunger-free America, an open mind and heart will always be good and fruitful companions.

In sharing these twenty-three essays I'm struck by the irony that the people I've interviewed and the places I've journeyed to may not speak the same "language" as me. What I mean is that terms like economic injustice, income inequality, or poetic imagination are not necessarily ones that come trippingly to their tongues nor how they would describe what they do. When Jo Argabright in Kansas says "I'm tired of watching my town die," or Maria Alonso in California says "This is my community, and I hear from the gardeners all the time how the 'garden makes us feel better,'" I hear two women giving voice to their needs, but more importantly those of others. Their expressions may be unencumbered by theory or an academic vocabulary, but their passions and frustrations don't mean that versions of theory and sophisticated word choices are absent from their thoughts. What drives them simply is the desire to make things better for others, a task we all know is immensely complicated.

Like many of the people I talked to, Dr. Nimali Fernando in Virginia is an intimate observer of the people and places she serves, in the same way that Gabe Pena keeps his finger on the pulse of his community in West Virginia. They both speak directly and thoughtfully of the failures of their respective systems, and they have each contrived extraordinary innovations to address those failures. Theirs is a deep knowledge of place and people formed over time from long-term immersion and experience. And while they are very individualistic and entrepreneurial by character, and to a degree charismatic, they choose the "we" pronoun over the "I," speak of partnerships and collaborations, and offer a vision that has been embraced by many others.

The rise of hunger across the US, growing as it does from a yawning economic inequality that plagues the nation, presents special challenges to local organizations who find themselves on the frontlines of vast community-based, hunger mitigation efforts. I spotlighted the food bank movement's earlier attempts to address the problem, akin to bailing out a leaky lifeboat before it succumbs to the rising water. Prior to that I described Seattle's Ballard Food Bank where the efforts of a united community were offering a diversity of services that held the promise of providing permanent solutions, not just band-aids. But even there, even with the aid of sophisticated, state-of-the-art client service methods and a generous community, there was an inchoate rage at the vast disparities in wealth that gave that region some of America's richest citizens, highest rents, but also a struggling underclass just scrapping by.

If it hasn't been amply highlighted throughout, I want to restate the importance of public policy as a critical pathway on our road to a hunger-free America. Sometimes it is big and rich (also known as big "P" policy changes), as in the changes advocated by Jan Poppendieck and others in the national school meal programs. These changes have brought better food to more children, but have taken decades to secure and more steps than anyone can count. More common and far less obvious are the small "p" (small policy) changes that may number in the thousands and often go unnoticed as policy actions. They would include the USDA Community Food Projects Competitive Grant program (currently funded at only $5 million annually), which enabled the Missoula (and hundreds of others communities across the nation) program to start and later expand. But also in Missoula, small "p" policy included decisions by public schools to develop gardening and food projects in collaboration with the private, non-profit Missoula project. In Paterson, local public policy actions in support of food are manifest in the development and retention of gardens and small food stores. The list goes on and would include one or more examples for every essay in this book. The point is simple: no matter how competent and dynamic the leadership is or how clear the cause, collaborations with government—our government, the one we elect—not just financially but fully integrated into its routine functioning, are necessary for real change to take place in our food systems.

There is a compelling moral argument that runs through justice theory and work that sometimes gets lost in their complex arguments. As I said at the beginning of this book, our first encounters with injustice often evoke an outrage, which itself grows out of our earlier moral foundations. People are hurt, people are suffering, people are oppressed and often left powerless in the face of harms imposed on them by other people, institutions, and systems. We turn to social and economic analyses to find explanations that often lead us to more theoretical constructions of justice such as Rawls's and the meta-analysis of sociologists like Putnam. But in the layering on of theory, often contained within the scaffolding of academia and echoed in the flat language of government technocrats who administer well-intentioned programs, the underlying moral sensibility can be diluted if not evaporated completely. To remain vigorous, to retain the underlying power of outrage and translate it productively into justice work we need to stay closely, even intimately in touch with the kind of people, places, and actions that I've highlighted in this book. In the words of Reverend William Barber, "We need a Moral Movement across the nation ... that is about the moral fabric of our society guided by a deeply moral and constitutional vision of what is possible."

As I bring this writing to a close, I see a nation, even a world, perched on the edge of social, cultural, and economic divides unseen since the nineteenth century. But it is more than my experience at work when I say that food and all of the activities and connections associated with the term food system are not only a gateway to change but also a path to mutual understandings and shared purposes. All of the essays here convey stories of people coming together, usually with a minimum of politics, to address a variety of food-related needs. The underlying principles of justice, when clearly stated and applied in a common-sense fashion have the capacity to win over the most recalcitrant of conservatives as well as skeptical liberals. Additionally, justice as a value and a compassion that resides in all of us can forge unities previously thought impossible. The principles of democratic participation, in the marketplace as well as government, are the bedrock of this nation that can never be taken for granted; increasingly they must be fought for every day. It may be a formidable task to scale the heights of the national policy making mountains, but at the local level where I have turned the spotlight for purposes of presenting countless opportunities, the entry points are many and the rewards can be great.

I've heard it said time and again that hunger and poverty will always be with us. Call it my innate sense of optimism as well as the immense progress I've borne witness to that makes me reject those who offer that bitter pill. I know the strength of the human heart and the tenacity of the human soul, and neither will relent until we indeed live in a hunger-free America.

REFERENCES

A Better Market. 2025. https://www.abettermarket.com (accessed March 13, 2025).
Agricultural Development Association – PARC. (n.d.). https://pal-arc.org/en (accessed March 13, 2025).
Alaska Department of Fish and Game. (n.d.). https://www.adfg.alaska.gov/index.cfm?adfg=divisions.subsoverview (accessed March 13, 2025).
Alaska Farm Tours. n.d. https://alaskafarmtours.com (accessed March 13, 2025).
Alaska Food Coalition. n.d. https://foodbankofalaska.org/alaska-food-coalition (accessed March 13, 2025).
Alaska Food Policy Council. n.d. https://www.akfoodpolicycouncil.org (accessed March 13, 2025).
Alaska Food Surveys and Reports. n.d. https://www.akfoodpolicycouncil.org/resources (accessed March 13, 2025.
Alaska Moose Federation. n.d. https://www.facebook.com/growmoremoose (accessed March 12, 2025).
Baldwin, James. 1961. *Nobody Knows My Name: More Notes of a Native Son*. Dial Press.
Balkenbush, Karolina. 2018. "Childhood Obesity Prevention and Treatment," *Today's Dietician* 20, no. 8: 52. https://www.todaysdietitian.com/newarchives/0818p52.shtml (accessed March 17, 2025).
Barber, Jesse and Adie Stone. December 31, 2022. Texas Food Access Study. https://static.texastribune.org/media/files/aa8d78c575b5e5667f659395cc2e4841/Texas%20Food%20Access%20Study.pdf (accessed March 13, 2025).
Barber, William J. II. 2016. https://archive.thinkprogress.org/rev-barber-moral-change-1ad2776df7c/ (accessed March 27, 2025).
Belluz, Julia. 2022. "Scientists Don't Agree on What Causes Obesity, but They Know What Doesn't." *The New York Times*. https://www.nytimes.com/2022/11/21/opinion/obesity-cause.html (accessed March 17, 2025).

Binational River Park. (n.d.) https://www.binationalriverfront.com (accessed March 12, 2025).

Bor, Jacob, Gregory H. Cohen, and Sandro Galea. 2017. "Population Health in an Era of Rising Income Inequality: USA, 1980–2015." *The Lancet* 389, no. 10077: 1475–90.

Bouchard, Claude. 2021. "Genetics of Obesity: What We Have Learned Over Decades of Research." *Obesity* 29, no. 5: 802–20. doi: 10.1002/oby.23116.

Bowens, Natasha. 2015. *The Color of Food: Stories of Race, Resilience and Farming*. New Society Publishers.

Case, Anne and Angus Deaton. 2020. *Deaths of Despair and the Future of American Capitalism*. Princeton University Press.

Centers for Disease Control and Prevention. 2021. Obesity National Health and Examination Survey. https://stacks.cdc.gov/view/cdc/106273 (accessed March 17, 2025).

Davidowitz, Esther. 2022. "Our Food Crawl. To 5 in 5 Blocks." Northjersey.com. https://www.northjersey.com/story/entertainment/dining/2022/11/04/palestinian-food-paterson-nj-restaurants-foodcrawl/65374170007/?fbclid=IwAR2d3siTL9Hqn9ZZ2Ow6w3JDWXlE2jlbFx8K8H7P4_6tVJqzI3Ktjy3gLLc#la357c2icozd13ozng (accessed March 13, 2025).

Dr. Yum Project. n.d. https://www.doctoryum.org (accessed March 12, 2025).

Edible Alaska. n.d. https://ediblealaska.ediblecommunities.com (accessed March 13, 2025).

Emerson, Ralph Waldo. 1957. *The Portable Emerson*. Edited by Carl Bode in Collaboration with Malcolm Cowley. Viking Penguin, Inc.

First Field. n.d. https://first-field.com (accessed March 13, 2025).

Grass Roots Garden Hub & Floral, Inc. https://www.facebook.com/grassrootsgardenhubandfloral (accessed March 13, 2025).

Hickman, Matt. 2022. "Binational River Park between Texas and Mexico Selects Overland Partners to Create Design Plan." *The Architect's Newspaper*. https://www.archpaper.com/2022/02/binational-river-park-between-texas-and-mexico-overland-partners (accessed March 13, 2025).

Huerta del Valle. n.d. https://www.huertadelvalle.org (accessed March 12, 2025).

Mills, C. Wright. 1959. *The Sociological Imagination*. New York: Oxford University Press.

New Jersey Development Authority. February 9, 2022. New Jersey Food Desert Communities. https://www.njeda.gov/wp-content/uploads/2022/02/Food-Desert-Communities-Designation-Final-2-9-22.pdf (accessed March 13, 2025).

Northjersey.com. n.d. "Paterson School District Approves $2M for Online Courses Amid Teacher Shortage." https://northjersey.com/story/news/paterson-press/2024/09/06/paterson-school-district-approves-2m-for-online-courses/75090355007 (accessed March 27, 2025).

Obesity Prevalence NHANES. https://search.cdc.gov/search/?query=NHANES&dpage=1 (accessed March 27, 2025).

Passaic County Food Policy Council. 2025. "About." https://www.unitedwaypassaic.org/passaic-county-food-policy-council (accessed March 17, 2025).

Pigeyre, Marie, Fereshteh T. Yazdi, Yuvreet Kaur, and David Meyre. 2016. "Recent Progress in Genetics, Epigenetics and Metagenomics Unveils the Pathophysiology of Human Obesity." *Clinical Science* 130, no. 12: 943–86. doi:10.1042/CS20160136.

Piketty, Thomas. 2014. *Capital in the Twenty-First Century*. Translated by Arthur Goldhammer. The Belknap Press of Harvard University Press.

Poppendieck, Janet. 2010. *Free For All: Fixing School Food in America*. University of California Press.

Putnam, Robert D. 2020. *The Upswing: How America Came Together a Century Ago and How We Can Do It Again*. Simon & Schuster.

Rawls, John. 1971. *A Theory of Justice*. Harvard University Press.

Ricard, Matthieu. 2023. *Notebooks of a Wandering Monk*. Translated by Jesse Browner. MIT Press.

State of Alaska, Department of Revenue (n.d.) Alaska Permanent Fund Dividend. https://pfd.alaska.gov (accessed March 17, 2025).

Taylor, Charles. 2024. *Cosmic Connections: Poetry in the Age of Disenchantment*. The Belknap Press of Harvard University Press.

Texas Health Institute. n.d. "2022–2023 Community Health Needs Assessment." https://texashealthinstitute.org/wp-content/uploads/2020/12/05-31-2023-Laredo-CHNA.pdf (accessed March 17, 2025).

Texas State Food Policy Council. 2023. https://capitol.texas.gov/tlodocs/88R/billtext/pdf/HB03323F.pdf#navpanes=0 (accessed March 17, 2025).

The Elephant Restaurant. n.d. https://theelephantbistrobar.com (accessed March 15, 2025).

Truly Living Well. n.d. https://www.trulylivingwell.com (accessed March 13, 2025).

Uncovering Rare Obesity. n.d. https://uncoveringrareobesity.com (accessed March 13, 2025).

Ward, Zachary J., Michael W. Long, Stephen C. Resch, Catherine M. Giles, et al. 2017. "Simulation of Growth Trajectories of Childhood Obesity into Adulthood." *New England Journal of*

Medicine 377: 2145–53. https://www.nejm.org/doi/full/10.1056/NEJMoa1703860 (accessed March 13, 2025).

Ward, Zachary J., Sara N. Bleich, Michael W. Long, Steven L. Gortmaker. 2021. "Association of body mass index with health care expenditures in the United States by age and sex." *PLOS One*. https://journals.plos.org/plosone/article?id=10.1371/journal.pone.0247307 (accessed March 17, 2025).

Wells, Pete. 2024. "I Reviewed Restaurants for 12 Years. They've Changed, and Not for the Better." *The New York Times*, August 6. https://www.nytimes.com/2024/08/06/dining/pete-wells-how-restaurants-have-changed.html (accessed March 17, 2025).

Williams, William Carlos. 1986. *The Collected Poems of William Carlos Williams, Volume I*. Edited by A. Walton Litz and Christopher MacGowan. New Directions.

Williams, William Carlos. 1988. *The Collected Poems of William Carlos Wiliams, Volume II*. Edited by Christopher MacGowan. New Directions.

Yesh Din (n.d.). https://www.yesh-din.org/en (accessed March 17, 2025).

INDEX

Able City 49, 52
Abu Ghazaleh, Saleem 84, 85
Adams, James Truslow 15
Adsit, Margaret 59
Agrarian Commons 44
Agrarian Trust 44
Alaska 57–62
Alaska Farm Tours 58
Alaska Farmland Trust 59
Alaska Food Coalition 62
Alaska Food Policy Council 58, 62
Alaska Permanent Fund Dividend (PFD) 62
Alonso, Maria 64, 65, 66, 199
Al-reef 84, 86
Amedeo, Joe 179
American Dream 15
Argabright, JoEllyn 128–33, 134–5, 199
Atlanta Food & Farm, LLC. 91
Atwood, Kansas 127–35

Bailey, Peggy 70, 71
Baldwin, James: "Nobody Knows My Name" 37–8
Ballard Food Bank, Seattle 69–73, 199–200
Barber, Reverend William 201
Berra, Yogi 174
Bethlehem Food Co-op, Pennsylvania 179
Better Market, A 34, 36, 38
Biden, Joe 48

Biden-Harris administration 161, 162
Bienvenidos Outreach Food Pantry 105
Binational River Conservation Park 51–3
Blanco, Palo 53
Boebert, Lauren 48
Bowens, Natasha: *Color of Food, The* 92–4
Brown, H. Rap 116
Buckingham, Bonnie 184, 185, 187

Campbell, Emily 134
Carter, Rubin "Hurricane" 28
Case, Anne 10
Castle, Jill 162
Celis, Mary 30, 33, 34–5, 36, 37
Chamberlain, Dr. Richard 50
Cheva-lean 151
Church, Don 59
Church, Michelle 59
Cigarroa, Melissa 48, 50–1, 52
Citizens United ruling 6
City Green 34, 35
City Market-Onion River Co-op, Burlington, Vermont 178, 179
civil rights movement 6
Civil War 14
Collins, Billy 172, 174
Community Food and Agriculture Coalition 184

INDEX

Community Food Innovation Center, Morgantown 43
Community Food Security Coalition (CFSC) 185, 186
Congress of Racial Equality (CORE) 110
Connecticut Fish and Game Division 151
Coombs, Susan 138
Cooper, Ann 140
COVID-19 34, 45, 53, 106, 121, 130, 131, 165–9
Crow, Jim 113
Cruz Ranch, Sapello, New Mexico 103–8
Cruz, Randy 103–8

Davidowitz, Esther 32
Davis, Deacon Willie 34, 35–6, 37
Davis Food Co-ops 180
De la Garz, Eligio "Kika" 186
"deaths of despair" 10
Deaton, Angus 10
diabetes 7, 79, 50, 155, 158, 160
Dietary Goals for the United States 145
Din, Yesh 82, 83, 86
Dixon Food Co-op 179, 182
Doctor Yum Project 98–101
Dole, Senator Robert 11, 144
Dorchester Food Co-op 182
Dream, The, Atwood, Kansas 130
Dylan, Bob 28

Elephant Restaurant, The, Hoxie, Kansas 127, 134
Elijah's Promise 122
Embry, Jim 109–16
Emerson, Bill 186
Emerson, Ralph Waldo 16, 18, 22
 American Scholar, The 5–6
Enos, Kamu 77, 78
Equal Exchange 84, 85, 124

Errichetti, Angelo 118
Evert, Robert 84, 124
Everts on p. 124

Facing Hunger Food Bank, Huntington 43, 46
Fernando, Dr. Nimali 97, 98–101, 199
FINI/GusNIP 186
First Field 120–6
FMLFPP 186
Food Bank of Alaska 62
food banks 11, 12, 40, 42, 61, 69, 151–4
 see also under names
food co-ops 177–82
food deserts 7, 33, 37, 47, 158, 161, 177, 179, 181
food injustice 6–7, 9, 12, 33, 81
food pantries 11, 33, 72, 105, 150, 169, 179, 184
food safety net 10–13
food stamps 11, 36, 62, 70, 71, 146, 150, 152, 186
food swamp 7, 33, 158
food system 6–9
Frank-Franco, Viviana 48–9, 50
Frost, Robert: "Mending Wall" 47

Garden City Harvest (GCH) 184–5, 187, 188
Garner, Eric 90
Georgia Farmers Market Association 92
Georgia Food Oasis 92
Georgia Food Policy Council 91–2
Georgia General Assembly 92
Georgia Organics 92
Good Foods Co-op, Lexington, Kentucky 179

Grass Roots Garden Hub, Kansas 134, 135
Great Depression 14, 72
Greene, Margorie Taylor 48

Habitat for Humanity 34
Hamilton, Alexander 31
Hanover Co-op, New Hampshire 180
Hartford Advisory Commission on Food Policy 194
Hartford, Connecticut, food banks 151–3
Hartford Food System 162–3, 173
Hawai'i 75–9
Health at Every Size (HAES) 158–9
Healthy Ontario Collaborative 64
Hernandez, David 178
Hightower, Jim 54
Hoover, Herbert 14
American Individualism 14–15
Huerta del Valle, Ontario 63–7

Jackson, Darryl 34
Jimerson, Misty 132
Johnson, Erik 43, 46
Juarez, Manuel 53
Juarez, Marcella 50, 53–4
justice, definition of 2–6

Kaiser Permanente 64
Kehayes, Steve 34
Kennedy, Robert F. 1
Khlifi, Sarra 62
King, Rev. Martin Luther 1
 assassination 29
 "I Have a Dream" speech 15
Kirkhart, Cyndi 46
Kiyabu, Derrick 76–7
Kostick, Marylynne 60, 61

La Montanita, New Mexico 178, 180
Laredo Center for Urban Agriculture and Sustainability 53
Laredo Food Policy Council 48, 49, 50, 53, 54, 55
Laredo, Texas 47–55
Last Crop, The (documentary film) 180
Leger, Patrick 120–3, 125, 126
Levine, Arthur 64–5, 66
Lexington Food Co-op 111
life expectancy 10
Lincoln, Abraham 13–14, 15, 139, 190, 193
Lohnes, Joshua 43, 46
Lorde, Audre: "Power" 89–90

MA'O Organic Farm, Oahu Island, Hawai'i 76–9
Main, Jeff and Annie 180
Mandela, Nelson 113
Manradge, Shana 34, 36, 37, 38
Márquez, Gabriel García: *Love in the Time of Cholera* 166
Martin, Lisa 34, 35
Marx, Karl 114
Matanuska Valley Tour, Palmer 59
McCarthyism 15
McGovern, Senator George 11, 143–6
Menendez, Bob 118
Mills, C. Wright 175
 Sociological Imagination, The 20, 174
Missoula Food Bank 184
Moonstone Farm 58–9

National Strategy on Hunger, Nutrition, and Health 161
Network Kansas 130
New Jersey tomatoes 117–26

New Roots Community Farm 39–46
Nixon, Richard 145
Nkromo, Kwabena 91–2
North American Free Trade Agreement (NAFTA) 49–50
Northeast Florida Food Bank 168
"Nourished Child, The" (website and podcast) 162
Nuri, Rashid 90–1

obesity 7, 40, 155–63
    childhood 98, 101, 156, 160–1, 163
    Laredo 50
Omidyar, Pierre 78
Orton, Tom 125
Oxfam 84

Palestinian Agriculture Relief Committee (PARC) 83, 84, 86
Palestinian olive farmers 81–6
Paradis, Julie 186
Park Slope Food Co-op, The, Brooklyn 178
Passaic County Food Policy Council 33, 35, 36
Paterson Great Falls National Historical Park 31
Paterson, New Jersey 27–38
PEAS Farm 184, 186
Peled, Miko: *General's Son, The: Journey of an Israeli in Palestine* 85–6
Pena, Gabe 40, 41, 42, 43, 46, 199
Piketty, Thomas 9
    Capital in the Twenty-First Century 9, 198
Pitzer College 64, 66
Pollan, Michael 99
Poppendieck, Dr. Janet 200
    Free for All: Fixing School Food in America 137–41
    Knee Deep in Breadlines 138
    Sweet Charity 138, 151
Puget Consumer Co-op, Seattle 178, 180
Putnam, Robert 9, 16, 198, 200
    Upswing, The 9, 10, 14

Quabbin Harvest Co-op 180

racism 7, 14, 28, 36, 90, 94, 110, 159
Rand, Ayn: *Atlas Shrugged* 15–16
Rawls, John 4, 5, 17, 18, 200
    principle of efficiency 4
    principle of fair equality of opportunity 4, 6
    principle of just savings 4, 5
    Theory of Justice, A 2–3, 4, 6, 8, 197
Reagan, Ronald 138, 151
Reconstruction 14, 15
Ricard, Matthieu 19
Rickford, Travis 131
Ridgewood, New Jersey 27–38
Rivera-Chapman, Christina 93
Rivera-Chapman, Tahz 93
Rogers-Jones, Kimmeshia 34, 35, 37
Roosevelt, Franklin Delano 14
Rotnofsky, Frank 52
Rutgers Cooperative Extension 122

Sacramento Food Co-ops 180
Salazar, Kenneth 51
Saleh, Bilal 83
Santa Fe Farmers Market 106, 167
Santa Fe Food Policy Council 173
Sayegh, Andre 31, 32, 33, 37
Schamberger, Courtney 131, 132
School Meals 11, 12
Second Harvest 150
September 11, 2001 2, 166, 167
Shtayyeh, Mohammad 86

Slotnick, Josh 184, 186, 187
Slow Food 111, 112
Social Security system, US 4–5
Society for Establishing Useful Manufactures (S.U.M.), New Jersey 31
Spaceship Looney-Tune 48
Stabenow, Debbie 192
Stone, Addie 54
Supplemental Nutrition Assistance Program (SNAP) 11, 35, 36, 42, 70, 71, 179
see also food stamps

taxation 4–5
Taylor, Charles 198
Thoreau, Henry David 125
Tierra Negra Farms 93
Title 42, 48
Today's Dietitian 161, 162
Touchpoints 101
Truly Living Well farm, Atlanta 90–1
Truman, Harry 138
Trump, Donald 48, 52, 191

USDA Community Food Projects Competitive Grant program (CFP) 67, 185, 186, 188, 194, 200

Vanderburg-Wertz, Darrow 179
Vietnam War 1–2, 15, 145, 159

Viggiano, Theresa 120–3
Vowell, Sarah 78
Unfamiliar Fishes 75

Walcott, Derek 19
Wallace, Henry 14
Walmart 46, 180, 181
Watkinson Community Garden, Hartford, Connecticut 190–1
Wells, Pete 13
Western Prairie Food Farm and Community Alliance 132
Wheeler, Susan 44
Whitaker, Daniel 93
White River Junction, Vermont 180
Whitman, Walt 8
Williams, Harrison 118
Williams, William Carlos 18
"Paterson" 29, 30
Winne Wellness Index 100
Winne, Mark: *Closing the Food Gap* 149–54
Winne, Peter 44, 168
Women, Infant, and Children (WIC) program 11, 12, 71, 162, 179

Yum Pediatrics 98–100

Zosel, Jean 186, 187